BOO-TICKLE TALES

not-so-scary stories for ages 4 to 9

"This silly and gently spooky collection of jumps, laughs, interactive moments, and mostly happy endings to satisfy the curious-for-creepy ages 4 to 9 set."
  —**Laura Packer,** storyteller and blogger

"An excellent resource for teachers, librarians, beginning storytellers, and teaching artists, to share this genre of stories in a learning environment with children 4 to 9 years old."
  —**S. Bunjo Butler,** librarian, storyteller, and a past president of the National Association of Black Storytellers (NABS)

"Lyn and Sherry have assembled a wonderful collection of 'weird but happy' stories that are fun to read and great for inspiring your own 'tickle' tales. Be afraid…but not too afraid!"
  —**Linda Gorham,** storyteller awarded the 2016 Distinguished Service Award from the National Storytelling Network

BOO-TICKLE TALES
not-so-scary stories for ages 4 to 9

Lyn Ford & Sherry Norfolk
Award-Winning Storytellers & Educators
Illustrations by Wendell E. Hall

Parkhurst Brothers Publishers
MARION, MICHIGAN

Parkhurst Brothers books are distributed to the trade through the Chicago Distribution Center, and may be ordered through Ingram Book Company, Baker & Taylor, Follett Library Resources and other book industry wholesalers. To order from Chicago Distribution Center, phone 1-800-621-2736 or send a fax to 800-621-8476. Copies of this and other Parkhurst Brothers Inc., Publishers titles are available to organizations and corporations for purchase in quantity by contacting Special Sales Department at our home office location, listed on our website. Manuscript submission guidelines for this publishing company are available at our website.

Printed in the United States of America

First Edition, 2017

2017 2018 2019 2020 12 11 10 9 8 7 6 5 4 3 2 1

Library of Congress Cataloging in Publication Data: Consult publisher website upon publication.

ISBN: Trade Paperback   978-1-62491-067-8

ISBN: e-book   978-162491-068-5

Cover and interior design by	Linda D. Parkhurst, Ph.D.
Proofread by	Bill and Barbara Paddack
Acquired for Parkhurst Brothers Inc., Publishers by	Ted Parkhurst

032017

DEDICATIONS

To the elders who gave me the gifts of stories
For the children who need and want those same gifts
and for the child's heart in all story-lovers
—*Lyn Ford*

To the loving memory of my poetry-reciting grandfather
who brought Little Orphan Annie to our house to stay,
and introduced us to the delicious thrill of being
just a little bit frightened while surrounded by
the warmth and security of his love.
—*Sherry Norfolk*

ACKNOWLEDGEMENTS

Thank you:

- Sherry Norfolk, my sistah-friend, who jumped into this project and laughed with me all the way to its completion.

- Ted Parkhurst, publisher and friend, for always believing that there's a book somewhere in my storytelling, and encouraging me to share it.

- The sadly missed and never forgotten Emil McVeigh, founder of the Storytellers of Central Ohio, who put me on stage to tell my first publicly-told ghost story.

- The National Storytelling Festival in Jonesborough, Tennessee, the Timpanogos Storytelling Festival in Orem, Utah, and the Haunting in the Hills Storytelling Festival in Big South Fork National Park, Tennessee, where my ghost stories were introduced to a national audience.

- Mary Shelley, Edgar Allan Poe, Bram Stoker, Saki, H.P. Lovecraft, Ray Bradbury, Shirley Jackson, Alfred Hitchcock, Boris Karloff, Bela Lugosi, Vincent Price, and all the other creatively creepy folks whose work touched my eyes, ears, mind, and heart.

- The Columbus Metropolitan Library system and its dedicated librarians, a resource beyond compare, whose venues often support my "Spookers & Haints" programs. Thank you, thank you, thank you!

- My dad, Edward "Jake" Cooper, who told some of the best silly to spooky stories I ever heard.

- My soul mate, Bruce Ford, whose patient, joyful dedication to my work of the heart is unbelievable and deeply appreciated, and our children, grandchildren, and great-grandchildren, who don't seem creeped out a bit by what I do. Love you all!

—Lyn Ford

Thank you to:

- Lynnie, my sistah-friend, who allowed me to join her on this project, and with whom I love to laugh and learn.

- Nancy Schimmel for her gracious permission to include my version of her delightful "Amy and the Crossnore" in *Boo-Tickle Tales*.

- Steve Floyd of August House Publishers for his generous permission to include "Billy Brown and the Belly Button Monster," which was published by August House as a hardcover picture book under the title *Billy Brown and the Belly Button Beastie*.

- Ted Parkhurst, for his support and constant, abiding presence in the storytelling community. Where would we be without you, Ted?

- The countless children whose spontaneous and honest responses have helped me craft my stories over hundreds and hundreds of tellings. Your attention and enthusiasm inspire and humble me.

- The love and light of my life, Sweet Bobby, who shared my delight in these stories and listened patiently as they progressed from rough drafts to final copy. May I never take your generous and loving spirit for granted.

—Sherry Norfolk

Table of Contents

INTRODUCTION

To Boo or Not to Boo…

"Technology does nothing to dispel the shadows at the edge of things."
—Neil Gaiman, author of the *Sandman* series and *The Graveyard Book,*
at TED 2014's "secret" Q & R session in Vancouver, B. C.

As a child in the 1950s, I did not even understand the word "technology." And I probably didn't care. The term was something I may have heard in some science fiction movies, or on the evening news of a growing cold war. For me, technology was Robbie the Robot in the 1956 movie *Forbidden Planet.* Technology was Wiley Coyote purchasing worthless inventions from a sinister company known as Acme in beloved Warner Brothers cartoons. Technology was the radar guns in the local department store's toy area for boys, which I visited often, and from which I acquired a set of Lincoln Logs, a cap pistol with a white "ivory" handle, a cowboy hat, and a sparking radar gun.

The word was created in the early seventeenth century, from the Greek *tekhnologia,* meaning systematic treatment. That word is rooted in the Greek word *techne,* meaning art or craft. All of that was important to me only because of a trademarked phenomenon we didn't have on our black and white television set, that marvel of the theaters, Technicolor. When I eventually saw *The Wizard of Oz* on my grandfather's television, then Disney's *Fantasia* on our boxy, brand new color TV…wow. Just, wow. I appreciated technology. But these stories couldn't compare in scope and power to the ones I heard from our family's storytellers.

Until, in 1958, a movie came out that I wasn't supposed to see. My older cousins in Franklin, Pennsylvania, told our parents they would take all of us little monsters to the movies to see—who remembers what they claimed we'd view? They left us sitting in the front row of the local debut of a British flick that had been released the year before. The movie was—dramatic music, please—*The Curse of Frankenstein!*

This was Hammer Production Company's first color horror film (I don't remember the term Technicolor™ being a part of that pronouncement, but the movie wasn't presented in black and white) with Peter Cushing as Dr. Frankenstein and Christopher Lee billed as The Creature. This flick had outraged reviewers and been critiqued as gruesome ghoulish, and horrible. When the movie began, my eyes were wide and attentive. But the music was loud and eerie, the screen too close. I remember keeping my eyes closed a lot of the time, but the squeals of my peers let me know that this was the most horrifying event of my entire seven years of life.

Why, oh, why, you ask, would my older cousins subject their little relatives to such terror?

They were teenaged girls and boys, meeting teenaged boyfriends and girlfriends, to smooch in the back rows of the theater balcony. We younger ones were their excuse to go to the theater. And there were enough of us within the same age group to make our parents giddy that the teenagers would get us out of my aunt's and uncle's house for two or three hours.

Now, I loved creepy programs, creepy stories, creepy poems. I crept downstairs to catch segments of *Alfred Hitchcock Presents.* I'd watched and mimicked Bela Lugosi speaking in strange syllables in *Dracula:* "Listen to them, children of the night. What music they make!" My dad told fantastic scary stories, and I was thrilled when he recited Edgar Allan Poe's "The Raven." It fascinated. I analyzed the art, considering the play of words, the light and shadow in films, the music and silences that made things seem bumpier in the night in viewed, written and spoken stories.

The crafting of such work didn't frighten me, for my great-grandmother had told me I shouldn't be afraid of things like ghosts.

"Dead folks don't bother you much," she said. "It's the livin' folks you need to worry about." The evening news always proved she was correct.

But Frankenstein's monster in color?!? This was my first truly frightening experience. I had no "systematic treatment" in mind for coping with what little I'd dared to watch on that movie screen. Years later, I would not watch the movie on television.

And, as an adult with sons who loved creepy tales, and a younger son and daughter who did not, I wondered…why had technology frightened the bejeebers out of me, when the scariest stories my father told had not?

Back to Neil Gaiman (2014) for the answer:

We have been telling each other tales of otherness…for a long time; stories that prickle the flesh and make the shadows deeper and, most important, remind us that we live, and that there is something special, something unique and remarkable about the state of being alive…

Fear is a wonderful thing, in small doses. You ride the ghost train into the darkness, knowing that eventually the doors will open, and you will step out into the daylight once again. It's always reassuring to know that you're still here, still safe. That nothing strange has happened, not really. It's good to be a child again, for a little while, and to fear—not governments, not regulations, not infidelities or accountants or distant wars, but ghosts and such things that don't exist, and even if they do, can do nothing to hurt us…

In order for stories to work—for kids and for adults—they should scare. And you should triumph. There's no point in triumphing over evil if the evil isn't scary…

Marveling in just being alive. Facing fear with a child's heart and in a safe environment. Triumphing over evil. Yep, those were the things I truly loved about my father's stories. I got to run into the darkness, to howl with the wolves in the woods or to conquer them, to peer into the shadows of the unknown, and to safely come home again—all within the realm of "this didn't happen." Always I was within the listening range of my dad's scary yet soothing voice and the warmth of his loving embrace.

That's a pretty good way to grow into the larger and real troubles of adulthood, isn't it?

But some kids just don't like scary stories, whether they're ghost stories or fairy tales or news reports. And that's okay, too. They're kids.

It is up to us, as the big people who love them, to be aware of our little people's curiosities, interests and real fears, and to be responsible enough to steer away from moments like meeting the Technicolor monsters. In 1958, my parents and aunties and uncles reprimanded the amorous adolescents who had acted so irresponsibly—hey, they were kids, too. That satisfied some of us, but left the potential for nightmares or running and jumping into parents' beds or other coping mechanisms coming into play. Two of my young cousins stayed up, chattering about the movie. I put little crawdads from the creek in my teenaged cousin's bedroom and went to sleep with a sinister smile on my face.

And I had crept out to the creek in my pajamas, tiptoeing in the darkness, wandering in the cool rippling water, alone and unafraid.

> Fairy tales, then, are not responsible for producing in children fear, or any of the shapes of fear; fairy tales do not give the child the idea of the evil or the ugly; that is in the child already, because it is in the world already. Fairy tales do not give the child his first idea of bogey. What fairy tales give the child is his first clear idea of the possible defeat of bogey. The baby has known the dragon intimately ever since he had an imagination. What the fairy tale provides for him is a St. George to kill the dragon.
>
> —G. K. Chesterton, *The Red Angel* (1909)

In words from someone who is far more connected to the educational aspects of scary stories than I:

> …scary tales serve an important purpose, say psychologists
> and children's literature specialists…[providing] great enter-
> tainment [and helping] kids through key developmental
> stages…fairy tales actually help kids face the fears they
> already have—and vanquish them."
> —Originally published by Patti Jones in the October 2001
> issue of *Child* magazine.

Thus, Sherry Norfolk and I offer to all those who love gentler squeals, giggles, and groans, a collection of stories to tickle with fearless frights: ***Boo-Tickle Tales.*** Within these pages, younger listeners, capable of enjoying stories for Pre-K through Grade Four, and those who love them enough to read stories with them and encourage reading and stories from them will find silly monsters, gentle ghosts, slightly spooky rhymes, and strange adventures.

Mentors, educators, parents, and story-lovers both young and young-at-heart will enjoy the discoveries, face the little fears, and find the giddy joy of racing through the darkness and stopping in the light.

These are not horror stories. Think of them as happy tales. Weird, but happy tales.

Lyn Ford

Whooo? Or Should We Ask, for Whooo-oom?

Boo-Tickle Tales are not-so-scary stories just right to be told or read to young listeners, Pre-K through fourth grade. Wait! What?? That's a wide age range, wildly diverse in terms of language skills, comprehension skills, attention spans, background knowledge, dominant learning styles—everything!! Yup, it truly is. So we've assigned each story an appropriate age range indication, based on our own extensive experience in telling these stories to thousands of kids. BUT—and this is a seriously big BUT—your experience with your specific audience is always your very best guide to what story is appropriate for them.

Baby Boos (PreK-Kindergarten)

Stirring and stirring and stirring her brew—wooooooo, woooooo!

Stirring and stirring and stirring her brew—wooooooo, woooooo!

Stirring and stirring and stirring her brew—wooooooo, woooooo!

Tip-toe, tip-toe, tip-toe—BOO!

Three, four and five-year-olds love the thrill of being just a little bit scared in a safe environment! My earliest memory of scary stories is my grandfather's recitation of *Little Orphant Annie* by James Whitcomb Riley (1885). As soon as my twin brother and I reached the mature and discerning age of three, our grandfather introduced us to Annie and the Gobble 'uns—and from then on we never stopped begging for him to recite it. He would delight in turning off the lights and gathering us on his knees…"and the Gobble 'uns 'll git you if you don't watch out."

Shivers! And giggles…we were safe in our grandfather's arms. Our stories for the Baby Boos are…

⊳ Short and repetitive, because the younger the listener, the shorter the attention span. The repetition is helpful for comprehension, vocabulary acquisition, predicting, and sequencing.

⊳ Interactive, because there is no one-size-fits-all answer to what approach will work best for individual children. Although different learning styles might develop as children get older[1], experts tell us that kids will generally learn in one of three ways:

Visual: Visual learners need to see in order to understand. You can help visual learners comprehend the story by using expressive facial expressions and body language. Repetitive, meaningful gestures help interpret new vocabulary and concepts. These kids probably won't make the physical motions that we suggest, but by watching you and the other kids do them, they will better understand the story.

Auditory: Auditory learners are best able to understand when they hear the story—but not if that story is being told or read in a monotone! We've indicated some of the ways your voice can be used to interpret the story, and added lots of sound effects that you and your small listeners can use to bring it to life for your auditory participants.

Kinesthetic: Kids with a kinesthetic learning style are the physically active members of the audience—you know the ones! They literally need to move in order to learn—and if productive, meaningful movement isn't provided, they will still need to move, but their choice of movement will likely be disruptive. Not their fault, it's the way they're wired! We've

---

1   "Diverse Learning Styles in Early Childhood Education" Posted October 16, 2012, in *Early Childhood Education.* http://education.cu-portland.edu/blog/early-education/diverse-learning-styles-in-early-childhood-education/

provided instructions for using gestures and movements that keep kinesthetic learners focused and help them comprehend the story.

> ▹ Fun—because it's hard to be frightened when your funny bone is being tickled! Laughter, play, and imagination help children cope with their fears, reassuring them that all is well.

Little Boos (First and Second Graders)

The worms crawl in, the worms crawl out,

The worms crawl everywhere 'round about…

If you've ever told slightly scary stories to this age group, you've heard plenty of squeals and screams. Little Boos love to be scared—especially when they are surrounded by friends and teachers, and all the lights are on! In a safe environment, children are able to master fears and difficult experiences by reinventing them in a playful way. Scary stories have the potential to support children's development by allowing them to vicariously meet and overcome danger while remaining firmly and completely safe.

Six and seven-year-olds are able to process longer, more complex stories with just a little more fright factor! Some of these stories offer opportunities for active participation. All of them offer opportunities for active imagination—actively visualizing the scenes in their minds—an essential comprehension skill. Our tales of monsters and goblins and things that go bump in the night will make Little Boos squirm, giggle, and gasp, but the sort-of-scary situations will always be resolved with a cheerful ending.

Big Boos (Third and Fourth Graders)

"Whoooooo's got my gooooooolden arrrrrrrrm?"

By the time my nephew was eight years old, he had watched the entire *Halloween* movie franchise multiple times without a single nightmare. He begged me for my scariest stories, scoffing when I refused to go beyond the limits that I had already drawn. "You'll have nightmares," I said. He and his dad disagreed, so I was finally persuaded, against my better judgment and with protests on file, to tell him a truly scary story: "Mr. Fox." Sean listened with a skeptical I've-heard-it-all-before look on his face—and woke his parents for the next three nights with nightmares.

This is a challenging age group! They love scary stories. They beg for scary stories. They long to be cool and mature and unflappable. But they aren't emotionally mature enough to handle truly scary stories yet. Many of these eight- and nine-year-olds have been watching horror movies for years, and they (and sometimes their parents) think that those movies prepare them for graphic content and blood and gore and guts. They don't!

Our Big Boo stories will make your listeners shiver just a bit. They'll conjure images, and they'll build spine-tingling suspense. But they'll end happily, and they won't create nightmares!

Sherry Norfolk

H-h-how? Tips and Techniques for Boo Tickle Tellers

Use Your Voice! (For all Boo Tickle Tellers)

Baby Boos, Little Boos, and Big Boos all delight in silly voices and sounds. If attention is wandering, a creaky *squeeeeeak* or deep **BOOM** is guaranteed to bring their focus back to the story. In addition, making character voices distinct helps listeners identify and visualize individual characters. They don't have to ask, "Who said that?" They know! (Keep in mind: If you're using a high squeaky voice, your listeners are not visualizing a huge and horrible monster!)

Don't know how to create character voices? In *Reading Magic: Why Reading Aloud to Our Children Will Change Their Lives Forever*[2], Mem Fox explains that there only seven things you need to do with your voice to expressively read or tell aloud:

- ▷ Speak HIGH

- ▷ Speak LOW (DEEP)

- ▷ Speak LOUDLY

- ▷ Speak SOFTLY

- ▷ Speak QUICKLY

- ▷ Speak SLOWLY

- ▷ Set the PAUSES

Used individually or in combination, these variations can create a

---

2   Fox, Mem. *Reading Magic: Why Reading Aloud to Our Children Will Change Their Lives Forever.* Harcourt, San Diego, CA, 2001. Chapter Six, "And Do It Like This," 39-52.

wide variety of voices. And yes, you CAN do this!

Let's look at HIGH—LOW. That refers to the pitch of your voice. Typically, your normal pitch is right in the middle of your voice range. It's the conversational voice you use when you narrate a story. You can vary that pitch by speaking in a much higher or lower range, and create distinctive character voices. It's sort of like singing, but you don't have to worry about carrying a tune!

Try humming up and down the scale to see just how much variety your voice already devises. Your speaking scale's notes are the range for your male voices, also good for big characters such as giants and ogres and monsters, and heavy footfalls thumping through the woods. At the high end of your speaking scale are the options for the smallest characters—such as a tiny fairy, a baby ghost, a little bat, or a creaking door. Try it—you'll find that you have at least three pitches—high, middle, and low—and probably lots more in between!

Now combine these high and low pitches with LOUD-to-SOFT. A deep, loud voice is perfect for the giant; to differentiate his character from that of a troll, give the troll a deep, soft voice (sort of menacing, isn't it?).

Now, add another element: FAST-to-SLOW. A deep, slow voice is just right for an ogre, since fast thinking and speaking are traditionally not qualities attributed to ogres. Faster thinking and moving characters (often the protagonists in folk and fairy tales) might be portrayed with medium range but quick speaking patterns. Really fast-speaking characters—like Li'l Loud-mouth—take practice!

SETTING THE PAUSES means giving your characters natural speech patterns. Are they hesitant and afraid? Then instead of saying, "Okay, let's go," they might say, "Okaaaay…let's go." While we've tried to indicate those pauses and speech patterns in the text ("Okaaaay"…meaning a slow stretching out of that last syllable, followed by a pause), you are certainly free to depict your characters as you see fit!

Practice and you'll find that those seven simple ways to use your voice can result in a multitude of options. And here's a trick for maintaining the character voices throughout the story: VISUALIZE! If mentally, you can see Li'l Loudmouth as you speak about him, you are less likely to mistakenly speak with Grandma's voice.

Expressive Reading and Telling

There is simply nothing more boring than listening to someone read or tell a story in a monotone. You wouldn't do that, right? Expressive voices interpret the text; they give it meaning, they help it come alive! Mem Fox's seven ways to use your voice apply to sharing expressive narration as well as to creating character voices. When the suspense is building, pace slows. Pauses increase tension, the voice becomes softer…and, perhaps, softer…to pull your listeners to the edges of their seats.

Using your voice effectively is a key skill when sharing *Boo-Tickle Tales.* Consider when to use soft, whispery voices—they can be really sinister! Also use conversational tones, loud voices, angry voices—and your storytelling will bring the tale to life.

Sound Effects

We've included LOTS of sound effects in these stories! Doors creeeeeaak, bats squeeeeeeeak, ghosts howl and moan and yowl! OOOOOOooooooooOOOOooo!

Sound effects are integral to telling scary stories! Try making those sounds—the kids will love 'em! Tell the kids to make those sounds with you—the kids will be totally engaged! Put your effort into not making those sounds, perhaps because you feel silly, or, maybe, you're concerned that your attempts will fail, and the story will fall flat. SPLAT! Get over your grown-up inhibitions, and let yourself play!

If you have trouble making the sounds, don't worry. First of all, No one will come to assess your endeavors and judge whether the sounds are precisely accurate. It's the effort that counts. And, in the second place, you can always ask the kids, "What sound would that make?" They'll be happy to do the work for you!

There's a Time and a Place

Keep in mind the types of tales you are sharing—*Boo-Tickle Tales*. These will not work as bedtime stories for every little story-lover. These may not even work for you as you get ready for a good night's sleep. The house doesn't have to be dark, the month doesn't have to be October, and the mood doesn't have to be that of the dark and stormy night. But, for the very first telling or reading of any of these stories, a quiet, cozy atmosphere, enough time to leisurely share, and the opportunity to talk a bit after the tales are told are requisites.

Once the kids have heard the tales, you can expect them to be requested any time of day. You may also expect to hear them retold by your child in his or her unique and satisfied way. Encourage your storyteller!

Lap-child tips
For Telling to the Littlest Ones, or Baby-Boo Sharing

The *Boo-Tickle Tales* that we've included for Baby Boos are short, repetitive, and funny, with lots of options for participation. While there are ghosts and witches and black cats and bats, they are not menacing or dangerous. These stories provide opportunities for you to talk with Baby Boos about what's real and what's not. They are a friendly introduction to the cast of characters that inhabit the scarier Big Boo stories.

Repeat, Repeat, Repeat

When sharing Baby Boo stories, some adults are tempted to skip the repetition: "And then they did it again." Please don't! Repetition is essential to Baby Boos—it builds comprehension and increases retention. As the repetitive episodes and phrases appear and reappear, you'll notice Baby

Boos beginning to repeat the phrases with you—actually beginning to tell the story! That could not happen if you skipped the repetitions!

And that's not all. The repeated episodes and phrases allow the listeners to practice recognizing the patterns within the story—and research tells us that the key to our intelligence is the recognition of patterns and relationships in all that we experience.[3]

Participation

Boo-Tickle Tales provide lots of options for participation—movements, sound effects, chants, rhythms, and songs. Note our use of the word options—these are not required, and certainly, we never force kids to participate! Offer the chance to participate, but allow the kids to determine what's right for them.

It's rarely necessary to give participation instructions before you tell the story—in fact, it's usually counterproductive. After five minutes of directions such as, "When you hear this, do that; and when I say that, do this," you've lost the audience. Not only are they bored, but they are often frustrated and confused. Rather, invite and explain participation when it naturally occurs within the story.

An example from "Amy and the Crossnore"

Amy knew about that, because she had done her homework. So every day when she took her goats up the mountain, she would sing a song to scare the Crossnore:

A-rum-pum-pum rhythm]	[Pat thighs once, clap 3x in
A-rum-pum-pum rhythm]	[Pat thighs once, clap 3x in
A-rolly-rolly-rolly-rolly	[Roll hands]

---

3   Schiller, Pam. *Start Smart: Building Brain Power in the Early Years.* Gryphon House, Beltsville, MD, 1999. "Patterns and the Brain," 85-93.

Rum-pum-pum!   [Pat thighs once, clap 3x in
rhythm]

As I sing the song for the first time, I model the actions and nod to kids to join in—that's all it takes. Then I invite them to sing: "Sing with her…" and we sing it again with actions. They've learned the song, and will join in every time it's sung after that.

Down underneath the mountain, the Crossnore would be
listening. He would hear Amy's feet go,

Pit-a-pat, pit-a-pat, pit-a-pat.   [Pat thighs in rhythm]

Positioning your hands ahead of time—as you say "he would hear Amy's feet go…"—cues the kids to mimic your movement; again, a simple nod of approval invites kids to join.

"OH NO, HERE SHE COMES!" he would roar.

He would hear the goats' hooves go,

Trip-trap, trip-trap, trip-trap.   [Tap two fingers in palm
rhythmically.]

Position hands as you say, "He would hear the goats' hooves go…" and they'll be ready to join in.

 "OH NO, OH NO, NOW SHE'S GONNA SING THAT
SONG!"

And sure, enough, he would hear Amy sing:

A-rum-pum-pum

A-rum-pum-pum

A-rolly-rolly-rolly-rolly

Rum-pum-pum!

At this point, they already know what to do and they do it! By modeling the desired participation and inviting kids to join in, you allow them to choose exactly the way and level they wish to participate. Some will sing but not move. Others will do the actions but not sing. Others will sing and do all of the movements. Still others will simply watch and listen and imagine. It's all good!

Vocabulary building

Your expressive voice and body language will also aid in comprehension. You are helping your listeners make meaning—and that's the key to literacy—being able to make meaning of the text, whether it is presented orally, in print, or through visual arts. Vocabulary acquisition is also increased when Baby Boos encounter new words in context, accompanied by eloquent gestures, facial expression and tone of voice.

Keys for Kid-Friendly Sharing
Little Boo and Big Boo Storytelling or Reading Together

You'll notice that there is a great deal of overlap between the Little Boo and Big Boo stories—and the choices you make will depend solely on your knowledge of the kids and how they will respond. But you can modulate the scarier stories to make them more Little-Boo friendly, and you can intensify the stories to make them more Big-Boo appropriate.

One of the easiest and most effective ways to modulate a scary story is to adjust your voice. Rather than the monster roaring, **"RRRRRRRRRR-RROOOOOAAAR!"** he can growl, "GRRRRRR." By losing the shock factor of a loud voice or sound, you can make the story more appropriate for Little Boos. For the Big Boos, it's usually okay to increase the excitement factor and make 'em jump!

Timing and pacing are vital to setting up jumps, creating mood, and developing suspense. "Jump" stories may be the only kind of storytelling in which you deliberately try to bore your audience—just for a few moments—in order to surprise them!

You can also modulate your actions. Big, wild gestures can be very disruptive, making Little Boos overly excited and inattentive. Lunging and grabbing at kids—even if they're your own kids—tends to illicit an over-reaction in response. And if they're NOT your own children, NEVER grab or touch! Lunge, yes. Grab, no. Even if it makes it scarier. No.

Creating Cozy Creepy Programs
From Libraries to Large Public Platforms

If you're planning to include a "scary" story in your program, plan ahead. "Scary" stories are a genre all to themselves. They are a little more risky to tell, and a lot more vulnerable to the values and beliefs of the audience (or the client). To avoid problems, learn as much as you can about your audience's ages, how your client feels about stories involving witches, ghosts, devils, haunted houses, etc. (whatever unnatural component or character is in your story), and consider how to adapt your story or program to their needs. Even if you've been asked to tell scary stories, it's still wise to ask those questions—do not assume anything! Your client will appreciate your consideration.

Telling the story

As with all stories, maintaining your own belief in a scary story is essential. It's a product of imagery...seeing and experiencing the story every time you tell it. Your belief and investment in the story will be reflected in voice, gesture, facial expression.

Does that mean you have to believe in ghosts? No. Does that mean you have to believe in the story? Yes. That story has to be real in your imagination in order to make it live in the imaginations of your listeners. You are creating a very special universe and atmosphere into which you are inviting your listeners to come, stay, and play.

Take, for example, "Turn Me Over!" Of course, you know that it ends with a joke—but if you giggle or smirk or give any hint of that as you tell the story, it's ruined. You have to live in that story and carry your listeners right along to the end.

And—even though this may seem contradictory to "live inside the story"—you must also watch the audience! Children's facial expressions and body language will tell you if they're truly frightened or if they're just having some spine-tickling fun. Pay attention, and adjust accordingly.

When I begin telling to a new group of Baby Boos, I use softer voices and sound effects until they become accustomed to the fact that weird sounds are going to come out of my mouth—and that they are allowed to join in on the weird sounds! As their comfort increases, my volume can increase as well!

However, if some kids are still looking frightened, or if I have a mix of Baby Boos with older listeners, I physically move away from the children who seem uncomfortable, creating a safe zone for them. That allows me to still do the scarier bits without making anyone cry!

And one more word of advice: Don't announce to the Big Boos that you are going to tell them scary stories—they will take it as a challenge to their maturity, and will feel compelled to tell you, "That's not scary! I wasn't scared!" even if they were terrified. Ack. Instead, try saying something like, "I'm going to tell you some *gross* stories—not scary, but definitely disgusting." Or, "I've got some interesting tales to share with you, some verrrrrrry interesting tales…" Then the big, tough fourth grade boys are totally willing to admit, "That was cool!" They may even say, "You scared me!"

Mwa ha ha!

Lyn and I offer these stories as a contribution to those who love to hear or read stories, and those who love to tell them. And as you read them, keep in mind that these tales are in the literary format, and are not a script to be memorized. We hope you enjoy the stories. We hope you want to share some of the stories, but share them in your own way, using your own words. Think of the versions in this book as food for thought.

If you choose to tell any of these stories, please give credit by name for your sources: Sherry Norfolk or Lyn Ford or both, the title of the book, **Boo-Tickle Tales,** and its publisher. The key word is "tell"—the authors have not given permission for their stories or original verses to be recorded or re-published in any format. For any consideration of those possibilities and permissions, you must contact the publisher well in advance of any plans.

Sherry Norfolk & Lyn Ford

Chapter 1
Creaky, Squeaky, Haunty Houses

Bad joke: What should always run around a haunted house? A big fence!

Too Noisy

By Sherry Norfolk

Baby Boos

Little Spider lived in a haunted house that she thought was too noisy, because the Daddy Ghosts howled, "WOOOOOO!"

And the Momma Ghosts yowled, "Wooooooo!"

And the Baby Ghosts cried, "Boo, boo, boo!"

"Too noisy!" said Little Spider, "I'm going to talk to the Wise Old Owl. He'll know what to do!" Off she went, creepy-crawl, creepy-crawl, creepy-crawl.

"Help!" said the Little Spider, "My haunted house is too noisy!"

"Go back," hooted the Wise Old Owl, "and put some bats in the house with you."

"Bats?"

"Bats!"

So the Little Spider went back, creepy-crawl, creepy-crawl,

creepy-crawl.

She put some bats in the haunted house, and they hung from the rafters squeaking, "Eee-eee-eee!"

And the Daddy Ghosts still howled, "WOOOOOO!"

And the Momma Ghosts still yowled, "Wooooooo!"

And the Baby Ghosts still cried, "Boo, boo, boo!"

"Too noisy!" said Little Spider, "I'm going to talk to the Wise Old Owl. He'll know what to do!" Off she went, creepy-crawl, creepy-crawl, creepy-crawl.

"Help!" said the Little Spider, "My haunted house is too noisy!"

"Go back," hooted the Wise Old Owl, "and put some black cats in the house with you."

"Cats?"

"Cats!"

So the Little Spider went back, creepy- crawl, creepy-crawl, creepy-crawl.

She put some black cats in the haunted house, and they meowed, "Mrooowwwwww!"

And the bats still squeaked, "Eee-eee-eee!"

And the Daddy Ghosts still howled, "WOOOOOO!"

And the Momma Ghosts still yowled, "Wooooooo!"

And the Baby Ghosts still cried, "Boo, boo, boo!"

"Too noisy!" said Little Spider, "I'm going to talk to the Wise Old Owl. He'll know what to do!" Off she went, creepy-crawl, creepy-crawl, creepy-crawl.

"Help!" said the Little Spider, "My haunted house is too noisy!"

"Go back," hooted the Wise Old Owl, "and put some witches in the house with you."

"Witches?"

"Witches!"

So the Little Spider went back, creepy-crawl, creepy-crawl, creepy-crawl. She put some witches in the haunted house, and they cackled, "Ah ha ha ha ha ha ha!"

And the black cats still meowed, "Mrooowwwwww!"

And the bats still squeaked, "Eee-eee-eee!"

And the Daddy Ghosts still howled, "WOOOOOO!"

And the Momma Ghosts still yowled, "Wooooooo!"

And the Baby Ghosts still cried, "Boo, boo, boo!"

"Too noisy!" said Little Spider, "I'm going to talk to the Wise Old Owl. He'll know what to do!" Off she went, creepy-crawl, creepy-crawl, creepy-crawl.

"Help!" said the Little Spider, "My haunted house is too noisy!"

"Go back," hooted the Wise Old Owl, "Take out the bats. Take out the black cats. And take out the witches."

"Really?"

"Really!"

So the Little Spider went back, creepy-crawl, creepy-crawl, creepy-crawl.

She sent the witches back to their cauldrons, "Ah ha ha ha ha ha ha!"

She sent the black cats back to their families, "Mrooowwwwww!"

She sent the bats back to hang in the trees, "Eee-eee-eee!"

And the Daddy Ghosts still howled, "WOOOOOO!"

And the Momma Ghosts still yowled, "Wooooooo!"

And the Baby Ghosts still cried, "Boo, boo, boo!"

"Ahhh!" said Little Spider, "My haunted house sounds just right!"

And she lived Happily Ever After!

BOO!

NOTES

Inspired by the noisy house in Margot Zemach's *It Could Always Be Worse: A Yiddish Folktale* (Square Fish, 1990), this haunted house is brought to life when the kids join in, howling and yowling and crying and creepy-crawling! The very repetitive text allows even very young listeners to learn the story as it is being told, to predict what is going to come next in the text, and to join right in!

This story is fun to act out in a classroom or library. Cast kids in the roles of Spider, Owl, Daddy Ghosts, Mama Ghosts, etc. Use everybody—you can cast several kids as each character. You'll narrate the story and let the kids say their lines or make their sounds and act out the story. Encourage the Spider to "creepy-crawl" and the bats to fly. You will have already modeled how those actions can look as you tell the story, so the kids will know how to do it appropriately.

Dramatization is not only fun, but educational! As they re-tell the story, the kids are demonstrating an understanding of sequence, setting, characters, problem, attempts to solve the problem, and resolution. If you have time, switch the roles around so that they are re-telling the story from different perspectives. Watch them problem-solve as they collaborate to tell the story.

The pattern of this story is so clear that it's easy to lead children in developing a whole new story using this story framework. It looks like this:

▷ Where will the new story take place? (Setting)

▷ What's the problem? Too Noisy (always!)

▷ Who thinks it's too noisy? (Main character)

▷ What three noises are causing the problem?

▷ Who is the Wise One?

▷ What three noises does the Wise One add?

▷ How does the problem get solved? Remove the last three noises— always!

Several years ago, a kindergarten class I worked with wrote their own story, "The Noisy Graveyard," and turned it into a play complete with costumes, props, and a backdrop. They put on their play for the entire school, proudly announcing that they had written themselves!

The Scary House

By Sherry Norfolk
Inspired by a Puerto Rican folktale

Baby Boos and Little Boos

Once there was a little girl named Nita who lived in a house that she thought was verrrry scarrrrry—because...

The floors went eee, awww, eee, aww. [With flattened hands parallel to floor, seesaw them like loose floor boards in time to the sounds.]

The doors went squeeeeak. [Use your forearm as a door with your elbow as the hinge.]

And the lights went SNAP! [Pull imaginary light cord.]

Every night, Nita's gramma took her up the stairs—*tap, tap, tap, tap.* [Pat thighs rhythmically.]

Down the hall—*eee, awww, eee, awww.*

To Nita's room, where...

She opened the door with a *squeeeeak!*

She turned on the light with a *SNAP!*

She pulled the covers up to Nita's chin.

And every night she said, "Now Nita, are you going to keep me awake with your moaning and groaning and crying like you always do?"

And every night Nita said, "Not me!"

So Grandma kissed her goodnight—*SMACK!*

She turned off the light—*SNAP!*

And she'd go back down the hall—*eee, awww, eee, aww.*

Down the steps—*tap, tap, tap, tap.*

And every night, she'd hear Nita say, "WAAAAAH!"

So Grandma would run up the steps—*tap, tap, tap, tap.*

Down the hall—*eeaweeaw.*

Open the door—*squeak!*

Turn on the light—*SNAP!*

And she'd say, "Nita, why are you crying?"

And every night, Nita would say, "Because I'm scared!"

One night, Grandma got a wonderful idea! "Nita, would you feel better if you had the dog to sleep in bed with you?"

And Nita said, "Uh-huh!"

So Grandma went back down the hall—*eee, awww, eee, aww.*

Down the steps—*tap, tap, tap, tap.*

She got the dog, and the dog and Grandma ran back up the steps—*tap, tap, tap, tap.*

Down the hall—*eeaweeaw.*

And the dog leaped into bed with Nita.

And the dog said, *"Woof, woof, woof!"* [Indicate a dog with begging paws.]

And Nita said, *"Ahhhhh!"* [Fold hands on chest.]

So Grandma kissed her goodnight—*SMACK!*

She turned off the light—*SNAP!*

And she went back down the hall—*eee, awww, eee, aww.*

Down the steps—*tap, tap, tap, tap.*

And she heard Nita say, "WAAAAAH!"

So Grandma ran up the steps—*tap, tap, tap, tap.*

Down the hall—*eeaweeaw.*

Opened the door—*squeak!*

Turned on the light—*SNAP!*

"Nita, why are you crying?"

And you know what Nita said? "Because I'm scared!"

"Nita, you already have the dog to sleep in bed with you—do you want the cat to sleep with you too?"

And Nita said, "Uh-huh!"

So Grandma went back down the hall—*eee, awww, eee, aww.*

Down the steps—*tap, tap, tap, tap.*

She got the cat, and the cat and Grandma ran back up the steps—*tap, tap, tap, tap.*

Down the hall—*eeaweeaw.*

And the cat leaped into bed with Nita.

And the cat said, *"Meow!"* [Indicate a cat with crossed paws held chest-high.]

And the dog said, *"Woof, woof, woof!"*

And Nita said, *"Ahhhhh!"*

So Grandma kissed her goodnight—*SMACK!*

She turned off the light—*SNAP!*

And she went back down the hall—*eee, awww, eee, aww.*

Down the steps—*tap, tap, tap, tap.*

And she heard Nita say, "WAAAAAH!"

So Grandma ran up the steps—*tap, tap, tap, tap.*

Down the hall—*eeaweeaw.*

Opened the door—*squeak!*

Turned on the light—*SNAP!*

"Nita, why are you crying?"

And you know what Nita said: "Because I'm scared!"

"Nita, you already have the dog and the cat to sleep in bed with you. Do you want the COW, TOO?"

And Nita said, "Uh-huh!"

So Grandma went back down the hall—*eee, awww, eee, aww.*

Down the steps—*tap, tap, tap, tap.*

She got the cow, and the cow and Grandma ran back up the steps—*tap, tap, tap, tap.*

Down the hall—*eeaweeaw.*

And the cow leaped into bed with Nita.

And the cow said, *"Moo!"* [Use your two little fingers to create horns on either side of your head.]

And the cat said, *"Meow!"*

And the dog said, *"Woof, woof, woof!"*

And Nita said, *"Ahhhhh!"*

So Grandma kissed her goodnight—*SMACK!*

She turned off the light—*SNAP!*

And she went back down the hall—*eee, awww, eee, aww.*

Down the steps—*tap, tap, tap, tap.*

And she heard Nita say, "WAAAAAH!"

So Grandma ran up the steps—*tap, tap, tap, tap.*

Down the hall—*eeaweeaw.*

Open the door—*squeak!*

Turn on the light—*SNAP!*

"Nita, why are you crying?"

And you know what Nita said: "Because I'm scared!"

"Nita, you already have the dog and the cat and the COW to sleep in bed with you. Now the only thing left is the stinky old PIG. You don't want that smelly pig in your bed, do you?"

And Nita said, "Uh-huh!"

So Grandma went back down the hall—*eee, awww, eee, aww.*

Down the steps—*tap, tap, tap, tap.*

She got the pig, and the pig and Grandma ran back up the steps—*tap, tap, tap, tap.*

Down the hall—*eeaweeaw.*

And the pig leaped into bed with Nita.

And the pig said, *"Oink, oink, oink!"* [Indicate a big belly with extended arms.]

And the cow said, *"Moo!"*

And the cat said, *"Meow!"*

And the dog said, *"Woof, woof, woof!"*

And Nita said, *"Ahhhhh!"*

So Grandma kissed her goodnight—*SMACK!*

She turned off the light—*SNAP!*

And she went back down the hall—*eee, awww, eee, aww.*

Down the steps—*tap, tap, tap, tap.*

[PAUSE]

BOOM!

So Grandma ran up the steps—*tap, tap, tap, tap.*

Down the hall—*eeaweeaw.*

Opened the door—*squeak!*

Turned on the light—*SNAP!*

And there was Nita—and the dog and the cat and the cow and the pig—but the whole BED had fallen apart. Grandma had to find a new place for Nita to sleep. So she picked Nita up in her arms, and she said to the critters, "Follow me!"

They all went back down the hall—*eee, awww, eee, aww.*

Down the steps—*tap, tap, tap, tap.*

To the new hall—*sh-sh-sh-sh!*

Where Grandma opened the new door with a *SHHH!* [Put your finger to your lips.]

She turned on the new light with a *SHHH!*

She pulled the covers up to Nita's chin.

And she said, "Now Nita, are you going to keep me awake with your moaning and groaning and crying like you always do?"

And Nita said, "Not me!"

So Grandma kissed her goodnight—*SMACK!*

She turned off the light—*SHHH!*

And she went back down the hall—SHHH!

Where she got into her own bed, pulled up her own covers and went to sleep. And Nita never again woke her up with her moaning and groaning and crying like she used to do, because now:

She didn't have a light that went *SNAP!*

She didn't have a door that went *squeak!*

And she didn't have a floor that went *ee-aww-ee-aw!*
So she was never afraid again!

NOTES

This popular cumulative Puerto Rican tale has been retold many times. Some sources are Laura Simms's *The Squeaky Door* (Random House, 1991), Judith Mathews and Fay Robinson's *Nathaniel Willy, Scared Silly* (Simon & Schuster, 1994), Pat Thomson's *The Squeaky, Creaky Bed* (Doubleday, 2003), and Margaret Read MacDonald's *The Squeaky Door.* (Harper Collins, 2006).

Every teller brings a personal flair to the story. I love the fact that it is so repetitious and offers so many participatory options—rhythms, gestures, sound effects, repeated phrases—that even the smallest Boo Babies quickly catch on and begin to tell the story right along with me.

When the Atlanta Children's Museum asked me for stories to help children get over their fears, this was the first one I turned to—a rollicking, noisy, silly answer to children's very natural fears of all those strange sounds in a darkened house.

The Little Boo Baby in the Big Fat Diaper

By Lyn Ford

Baby Boos, Little Boos, and Big Boos

Trick or treat night had begun! Big Brother, Big Sister, and Little Sister walked through the neighborhood. They carried big paper bags for all the treats they might get at neighbors' houses: candy and pencils and candy and stickers and candy and candy and candy.

Big Brother was dressed as a pirate. Every now and then, he would stop walking, straighten his big black hat, adjust his eye patch, raise his plastic cutlass, and shout, "Yo HO!"

Big Sister was dressed like a princess. Every now and then, she would stop walking, smooth her silky skirt, fix the shiny crown on her head, and give a royal wave as she proudly said, "Everybody *loves* princesses!"

Little Sister wore the hand-me-down teddy bear suit that her big brother and sister had worn when they were her size. Every now and then, she would stop walking, scratch her teddy-bear neck, scratch her teddy-bear belly, scratch her teddy-bear tail, and shout, "This thing itches!!!"

Big Brother and Big Sister laughed and kept on walking toward the next house on the block. Then Little Sister yelled, "Hey! You not supposed to walk away from me! I'm da baby, remember? You supposed to walk wif me! Mommy said you supposed to walk wif me! Mommy said—HEY! YOU SUPPOSED TO WALK WIF ME! YOU SUPPOSED TO BE WATCHIN' OVER ME! HEY! I'M DA *BABY!*"

Big Brother and Big Sister laughed and ran to the next house, where they sang, "Trick or treat, smell my feet, give me something good to eat!"

And even though that was a disgusting song, they received lots of treats.

Little Sister just held out her treat bag and said, "Thank-oo very much!" She got more treats than her brother and sister.

When their bags were full and heavy, Little Sister said, "Time to go home!"

But Big Brother and Big Sister kept walking. There was one more house on the block.

It was dark and gloomy. No porch light shone for them. The shutters rattled at every window, and the wind whispered through broken window-panes. This was the house all the children had been told not to visit. This house was supposed to be…haunted!

Little Sister scratched at her teddy-bear ears. "Hey," she said, "Hey, where we goin'?"

"To get more candy," Big Brother said.

"Hey, we not supposed to go to that house!" cried Little Sister.

"Then don't go," Big Sister said. "Go home. We're going to get more candy."

Little Sister stood alone as the streetlights began to glow. She scratched, she scratched a lot. Then she yelled, "HEY! YOU SUPPOSED TO BE WIF ME! YOU SUPPOSED TO BE WATCHIN' OVER ME!" And she ran after her brother and sister.

They stood in front of the dark and gloomy house. Big Brother said, "You two wait here. I'm not afraid. After all, I'm a pirate. Yo-HO!"

Big Brother walked up the front porch steps—creaky, creaky, creaky crack—then across the porch—squeaky, eeky, squeak—and then he reached out and opened the old and rotting wooden door—eee-eee-eee-e.

Big Brother sang, "Trick or treat, smell my feet, give me something good to eat!"

In the moonlight that shimmered through a hole in the wall, Big Brother saw something floating at the top of the stairs that led to the second floor. Something pale and as shimmery as the moonlight.

It was a Big…Boo…DADDY! OOOOH!

Behind it was a Big…Boo…MOMMY! OOH! OOH!

And behind them both was a Little…Boo…BABY, in a big fat diaper.

The Little Boo Baby rolled right through the Big Boo Daddy and the Big Boo Mommy. It bounced down the steps on that big fat diaper, rushed toward Big Brother, stuck out its tongue, and said, "Thhhpf."

"YA!" yelled Big Brother. He fell out the front door. He dropped his bag of treats on the porch. He leaped down the stairs, and he ran home.

The door to the old house creaked shut—eee-eee-eee-e.

Big Sister looked at Little Sister. Little Sister looked at Big Sister. Little Sister watched Big Brother running down the street. Little Sister yelled, "HEY! YOU SUPPOSED TO BE WIF ME! YOU SUPPOSED TO BE WATCHIN" OVER ME!"

Big Brother lost his pirate hat and dropped his cutlass. He threw the patch off his eye. He yelled, "YA!" and he kept running.

"Hmpf," muttered Big Sister. "That was very silly behavior for a pirate. I'll get some candy, and no one will try to scare me. After all, I'm a princess. Everybody *loves* princesses!"

Big Sister walked up the front porch steps—creaky, creaky, creaky crack—then across the porch—squeaky, eeky, squeak—and then she reached out and opened the old and rotting wooden door—eee-eee-eee-e.

Big Sister sang, "Trick or treat, smell my feet, give me something good to eat!"

In the moonlight that shimmered through a hole in the wall, Big Sister saw something floating at the top of the stairs.

It was a Big…Boo…DADDY! OOOOH!

Behind it was a Big…Boo…MOMMY! OOH! OOH!

And behind them both was a Little…Boo…BABY, in a big fat diaper.

The Little Boo Baby rolled right through the Big Boo Daddy and the Big Boo Mommy. It bounced down the steps on that big fat diaper, rushed toward Big Sister, stuck out its tongue, and said, "Thhhpf."

"MA!" yelled Big Sister. She fell out the door. She dropped her bag of treats on the porch. She tripped down the stairs, and she ran home.

The door to the old house creaked shut—eee-eee-eee-e.

Little Sister looked at the door. Little Sister watched Big Sister running down the street. Little Sister yelled, "HEY! YOU SUPPOSED TO BE WIF ME! YOU SUPPOSED TO BE WATCHIN' OVER ME!"

Big Sister lost her crown. She tripped over her skirt. She yelled, "MA!" and kept running.

Little Sister was all alone in front of that dark and gloomy house.

She scratched her teddy-bear shoulder. She scratched her teddy-bear elbow. Then she said, "Well, I might as well see what scared my sister and brother."

Little Sister walked up the front porch steps—creaky, creaky, creaky crack—then across the porch—squeaky, eeky, squeak—and then she reached out and opened the old and rotting wooden door—eee-eee-eee-e.

Little Sister didn't sing. She held out her treat bag and said, "Hey! Thank-oo very much!"

In the moonlight that shimmered through a hole in the wall, Little Sister saw something floating at the top of the stairs.

It was a Big…Boo…DADDY! OOOOH!

Behind it was a Big…Boo…MOMMY! OOH! OOH!

And behind them both was a Little…Boo…BABY, in a big fat diaper.

The Little Boo Baby rolled right through the Big Boo Daddy and the Big Boo Mommy. It bounced down the steps on that big fat diaper, rushed toward Little Sister, stuck out its tongue, and said, "Thhhpf."

Little Sister stared at the Little Boo Baby. She stared at that big fat diaper. She sniffed, *sniff.* Then she said, "Ewww. Wait a minute, baby. I will be right back!"

Little Sister ran out the door, and across the porch, and down the steps, and to her home. But Little Sister came back, with her mommy.

Little Sister still carried her trick or treat bag. Mommy carried a bag, too, an old blue bag with a shoulder strap. It wasn't for gathering treats on trick or treat night.

The door to the dark and gloomy house was still open. Hand in hand,

Mommy and Little Sister walked toward the front porch steps. They walked up the steps—creaky, creaky, creaky crack—then across the porch—squeaky, eeky, squeak—and then through the open, old and rotting wooden door.

Little Sister and Mommy didn't sing. They didn't speak, because…

In the moonlight that shimmered through a hole in the wall, Little Sister and Mommy saw something floating at the top of the stairs.

It was a Big Boo DADDY! OOOOH!

Behind it was a Big Boo MOMMY! OOH! OOH!

And behind them both was a Little Boo Baby, in a big fat diaper.

The Little Boo Baby rolled right through the Big Boo Daddy and the Big Boo Mommy. It bounced down the steps on that big fat diaper, rushed toward Little Sister and Mommy, stuck out its tongue, and said, "Thhhpf."

Mommy sniffed. Then Mommy smiled at the Little Boo Baby in the big fat diaper. Then Mommy reached into her old blue bag and pulled out a baby wipe, a bottle of baby powder, and a fresh, clean diaper.

And without one bit of fear, Mommy changed that big fat diaper.

Well, the Big Boo Daddy floated down the steps and said, "OOOOH! Thank you! We ran out of diapers!"

The Big Boo Mommy floated down the steps and said, "OOH! OOH! Thank you! Thank you! Thank you!"

And the Little Boo Baby in the fresh, clean diaper said, "Thhhp-fank-oo very much!"

Little Sister, still holding her trick or treat bag, laughed and said, "HEY! You welcome!"

And, suddenly, from nowhere at all, candy fell into Little Sister's bag! "Oooh, Thank-oo very much!" she said to the Boo family.

Then Little Sister and Mommy carried their bags out the door. It closed behind them—eee-eee-eee-e. They picked up the treat bags left on the porch by Big Sister and Big Brother.

Trick or treat night was over.

NOTES:

This story has been a favorite to tell since I created it more than twenty-five years ago. It is a participatory tale, with my story-helpers repeating the dialogue for Big Brother, Big Sister, Little Sister, and the Boo family. Story-helpers also re-create the sounds of the shutters rattling (patting on their legs), the wind whispering ("Shhhhh"), the front porch steps creaking, the porch floorboards squeaking, and the wooden door slowly opening. When each of the parent Boos speaks in ghostly fashion, the children wiggle their fingers. When the Little Boo Baby sticks out its tongue, well…and yes, that "Thhhpf" is a spitting sound.

The story reinforces using common sense and empathy, virtues that have become essential in my playshops with children young and old. And Little Sister? I've always loved making creative, intelligent little kids with big voices the heroes in stories.

Jack Meets Jeffie Boo-Bottom

Adapted by Sherry Norfolk

Big Boos

Jack and his momma were very poor. They lived in a tiny little shack and wore raggedy clothes. They didn't have much food, they didn't have any money to buy food, and neither one of them had a job to EARN any money to buy food.

One day Jack announced, "Momma, I'm going to go find me a job."

His momma looked at Jack with a look he had seen many times. It said, "Hmph!" And Jack knew why—because he had never done a bit of work in his life. But he hurried on.

"I know that you know that I'm sort of lazy, Momma, but I really will find me a job!" Jack claimed. "And I'll work hard and bring home some money so we can eat. You'll see, Momma, you'll be proud of me!"

His momma gave him that same look—"Hmph!"—but then she smiled and gave him a big hug. "I'm proud that you thought of it, Jack, and I'll be waiting right here when you come home."

Jack's momma wrapped up the last little bit of food they had left—some dried-up cornbread and a jar of buttermilk—and gave it to Jack. "You take care of yourself, now, you hear?" she told him with a sob, and Jack went off to seek his fortune.

He walked and he walked, uphill and downhill, through the forest and into a clearing, across a stream and into the village. It was oh-dark-thirty by the time he started along the main road. In the dusky evening light, he saw an old man hobbling down the road towards him.

"Howdy, Sir," said Jack politely. "My name's Jack, and I'm looking for a job. Do you have any work for me to do?"

"Well, hello there, Jack," said the old man. "I sure do! You see that big house up on the hill yonder?" The old man pointed to a sinister-looking house that must have been abandoned for a hundred years. The windows were broken, the paint was peeling, there was a hole in the roof, and weeds stood as tall as Jack in the yard.

"You mean that haunted house?" asked Jack.

"Haunted! How did you know it was haunted?" asked the old man.

"Well, anyone can see it's haunted," Jack answered. "What about it?"

"Well, the haunting is the problem, son! That house belongs to me, but nobody has been able to live in it for a hundred years because of the ghost of Jeffie Boo-Bottom. But Jeffie Boo-Bottom will have to go away and never come back if someone can spend the entire night in that house without being scared clean out of their wits by morning. So I need you to go up there and spend the night. If you can do that, the haunting will end and I will give you the house and a hundred dollars, besides."

Well, that was just the kind of job Jack was looking for! No work, just sleeping through the night and waking up with a hundred dollars and a new house!

"Alright, Sir, I'll do it," he announced. So the old man gave him the skeleton key, and Jack climbed on up the hill. He fought through all the weeds in the yard and tip-toed carefully across the rotten porch and let himself in.

Squeeeeeeeaaaaaaaak! That door gave a creak like a witch's cackle. Jack jumped.

"Hmph. No squeaky old door is gonna scare me clean out of my wits."

Jack looked around. Except for the huge cobwebs and the thick coat of dust, it looked like a normal house. There was a nice enough parlor, with a big fireplace and a stack of firewood. Jack shivered a little in the shadowy gloom.

"Good! I'll just make a fire!" he decided.

He reached up into the chimney to open the flue. He felt around until his hand touched something cold and clammy, and he gave it a YANK—*scrooooooooooonk!* Something rained down on Jack's head and shoulders!

Jack backed away from the hearth on all fours just as fast as he could. He had yanked the flue open, and a shower of filthy ash had fallen out.

"Hmph," he said, "No dirty old chimney is gonna scare me clean out of my wits. I'm gonna build a nice warm fire and eat my supper. "

But he didn't build a fire because a hair-raising sound had begun to come from far up in that fireplace:

"MWA HA HA HA HA! HEH HEH HEH HEH HEH! HEE HEE HEE HEE HEE!"

Maniacal laughter filled the house, echoing around the empty rooms and making Jack's head seem to vibrate like a bell. Then suddenly, a ghost swished down the chimney and into the parlor—WOOOOSH!

The ghost was still laughing its spine-chilling laugh, "MWA HA HA HA HA! HEH HEH HEH HEH HEH! HEE HEE HEE HEE HEE!"

Jack stuffed his fingers in his ears and stared at the filmy white apparition. It wouldn't stay still—it was gyrating all over the room, twisting and turning, flipping its ears and flopping its elbows, dancing a crazy dance and grabbing at Jack's hair every time it passed by.

And all the while, the laughter never stopped.

"MWA HA HA HA HA! HEH HEH HEH HEH HEH! HEE HEE HEE HEE HEE!"

And all the while, tiny cloudy wisps of ghostly drapery whirled off and away from the ghost.

Jack ducked and covered his head, but the ghost kept snatching at him, pulling at his arms, yanking at his hair.

"No evil old laughter is gonna scare <u>me</u> clean out of my wits!" yelled Jack over the deafening laughter. "Why don't you just quit that racket?"

The laughter stopped, but Jack's ears kept ringing. He was shaking his head to make the ringing stop when the ghost began to writhe and moan, swooping right up into Jack's face and twisting its own face in a horrid, horrible grimace. A long ghostly tongue stuck out and waved around, and the putrid smell of the grave came from its mouth.

"WOOoooooooooooooOOOOOOOOOOO! OOOooooooooooooo oooOOOOOOoooooooo!"

"No ugly old faces are gonna scare <u>me</u> out of my wits!" Jack yelled, and he made an even uglier face right back at the ghost.

Startled, Jeffie Boo-Bottom jerked away, leaving more wisps of hazy ghostly mist behind. Jack watched as the ghost tried to pull himself back together. Then Jack got an idea.

"Hey, you! Jeffie Boo-Bottom! You're a pretty good dancer. Why don't we have a dance contest?" Jack said. "If you win, I'll leave and never come back. If I win, you'll leave and never come back. What do you say?"

"MWA HA HA HA HA! HEH HEH HEH HEH HEH! HEE HEE HEE HEE HEE!" shrieked the ghost. "How do we decide who has won?"

"The last one left standing is the winner!" Jack explained.

"HEE HEE HEE HEE HEE! That will be ME!" howled the ghost—and he swirled off into his wiggling, jiggling, wriggling, writhing dance. Bits and pieces of misty, smoky ghostly tendrils spun off the gyrating figure.

Jeffie Boo-Bottom shook his big ghostly bottom and thrashed his ghastly arms and wailed his ghostly wail.

"WOOoooooooooooooOOOOOOOOOOOO!   OOOoooooooooooooo oooOOOOOOooooooo!"

Bigger pieces of ghostly gunk began to fly all over the room! Jack stood still and watched as the ghost danced itself smaller and smaller and smaller and…

POOF!

The dancing and the wailing and Jeffie Boo-Bottom all vanished— disappearing into thin air.

Jack finished building and lighting the fire. He ate his dinner and went to sleep. And in the morning, the old man signed over the deed to the house and handed Jack a hundred dollars!

Jack set off for home. When his momma saw him coming home empty-handed she gave him that look—hmph!—but when he told her what had happened she gave him a great big hug.

"I always knew you were a clever boy, Jack!"

Jack and his momma moved into that old house and fixed it up, and they lived there ghost-free happily ever after.

NOTES:

This story was inspired by "Jack and the Haunted House," an Appalachian folktale in which Jack encounters a skeleton falling down the chimney bone by bone and demanding that Jack find its skull. Jackie Torrence told it back in the day. Elizabeth Ellis published it in *Ready-to-Tell Tales* by David Holt & Bill Mooney (August House, 1994), and Bobby Norfolk tells his own version. A picture book version by Robert D. San Souci called *The Boy and the Ghost* (Simon and Schuster, 1989) gives it a little bit different twist.

"Jack and Jeffie Boo-Bottom" also took inspiration from Cynthia D. DeFelice's *The Dancing Skeleton* (NY: Macmillan, 1989), in which an ornery dead man refuses to stay in his coffin. His skeleton dances itself to pieces when the best fiddler in town comes to call on his widow.

You see where the ideas came from? A little bit of this (Jack and a Haunted House) + a little bit of that (a haint that falls apart) x (a lot of imagination) = A NEW STORY!

Give this a try! Write your own Haunted House story by completing this outline:

- ▷ What is haunted? (House, cavern, attic, cellar…?)

- ▷ Who goes in?

- ▷ Why does that character go in? (What's the motivation?)

- ▷ What is haunting the house? (Ghost, witch, goblin, ghoul…?)

- ▷ What happens to people who try to stay in the house? (They get eaten, frozen, dissolved…?)

- ▷ How can the haint be banished?

- ▷ How does the story end? (Does the protagonist get rewarded somehow? Does she/he get in trouble for trespassing…?)

Voila! You've made up your own story! Now embellish it by adding lots of details that help your reader or listener visualize the characters, setting, and actions. Practice creepy character voices and sound effects and tell it to a friend on a dark and stormy night!

Li'l Loudmouth

By Lyn Ford

Big Boos

Sometimes, we hear sounds that annoy us, like loud voices and too much talk. Sometimes, we hear odd noises that make us a bit nervous, but, if we listen long enough, we realize they're sounds we know. The old clock ticking in the hallway. The wind rattling tree branches. The dog or cat or hamster, wide awake and ready to play. The voices of folks in our family.

But, sometimes, there are sounds that we can't identify, and as we listen…listen long enough…we realize…we don't recognize the sounds at all.

One sound all the cousins knew was the voice of their littlest cousin. He was very loud, and he spoke very quickly so that all his words blended into one long, obnoxious noise:

HiCanwegointhewoodsthisafternoonbecauseIneedtosee
ifIcanfindsomeleavestopressbetweentwopiecesofwaxed
paperandtaketoschooltomorrowtoidentifyinscienceclass…

Nobody was sure what he was saying most of the time. But they knew that, whatever he said, he said too quickly and too loudly. The only one who understood him was Grandmother, but she usually said, "Honey, slow down! And speak a little softer. You have such a loud mouth!"

So the older cousins nicknamed that noisy little cousin "Li'l Loudmouth". And they tried their best to be someplace else whenever he came around, which was very difficult. Older cousins are often asked to watch over little cousins, especially when they're all visiting at Grandma's house.

One warm autumn Saturday, when the wind was rustling the last leaves from the trees, the older cousins sat on Grandma's front porch. They couldn't think of anything to do, couldn't find any games to play, or books to read, and Grandma didn't have a TV. Nope, nothing to do. That usually led to some silly argument about who could throw a ball the farthest or who could run the fastest or who was the biggest scaredy-cat.

And *that* usually led to Grandma finding some chores around her house for them all to do, or sending them all on an errand.

Sure enough, a competition had begun over which one of the cousins could jump farthest from the top of the porch steps. And Grandma came onto the porch with a stern face and money in her hand. She commanded, "Go to Warren's Market and get me some laundry detergent. Get the kind in the dark blue box. Thank Mr. Warren for it, and use the change to get yourselves some candy. Watch out for the littlest one, and share that candy, you hear? Now, GO!"

Into the house went Grandma. Off the porch ran the cousins, the big ones in front of the littlest one, Li'l Loudmouth.

Li'l Loudmouth shouted,

HEYyouarerunningtoofastIcan'tkeepupandyou'resupposedtowatchoutformeHowcanyouwatchovermewhenyou'reallinfrontofmeHEYAREYOULISTENINGTOME?

They weren't listening. They were running as quickly as they could, down the hill past the neighbors' houses and across the baseball field to Mr. Warren's little market.

The big cousins got to the neighborhood market, bought the laundry detergent in the dark blue box, and said thank you to Mr. Warren, who helped them count chocolate drops and red licorice sticks and bubble gum. They thanked Mr. Warren again and left the store.

As they divided the candy, they heard a voice coming across the baseball field and toward them. They recognized it:

HEYyougotthedetergentdidyouremembertothankMr.

WarrenISTHATCANDYINYOURHANDSRememberyou're-
supposedtoshareitwithmebutdon'tgivemeanybubblegumIt-
sticksinmyteethandmakesmeburprealloudburpslikethis
BURP!

Ack. Li'l Loudmouth.

As they gave Li'l Loudmouth three sticks of red licorice and told him he had to chew each bite thirty times, the big cousins began to whisper. Li'l Loudmouth chewed, unable to speak, which gave the cousins a chance to tell him what they were going to do.

"We're not gonna eat any of the rest of this candy," said Wilmer, the biggest cousin. "We're gonna give it all to you, "Li'l Loudmouth, if—*if*—you can stay in the old Dobbs House until the sun goes down."

"MgldDbbsmff?" asked Li'l Loudmouth. Then he swallowed the licorice. And, for once, his bigger cousins understood every *loudly, clearly pronounced* word he said.

"The old Dobbs House? Guys, that place is *haunted!*"

"Aw, it's not haunted. People just say it's haunted. What's the matter? You scared?"

Li'l Loudmouth didn't know which cousin spoke. His eyes were closed and he was speechless, just thinking about the old Dobbs House, a creaking, abandoned monster of a place just beyond the woods behind Grandma's house.

"Well, if you're too scared to stay there until sundown, then you don't get all this candy," taunted Wilmer. "All this delicious candy."

Li'l Loudmouth clearly said four words, "Okay. I'll do it."

The older cousins walked Li'l Loudmouth past Grandma's house, down the winding path that led around the wooded area behind her tidy yard, past the huge, ancient trees that set everything in shadows, and up the crooked steps to the porch of the old Dobbs House.

They didn't go inside. They shoved Li'l Loudmouth toward the rickety open door. Then Wilmer shook the bag of candy under Li'l Loudmouth's nose. "Go on, go on in. At sundown, come to Grandma's, and you'll find the candy waiting for you on the porch."

Li'l Loudmouth went in…one…tiny…step at a time. When they couldn't hear his footfalls anymore, the big cousins started to fidget.

"You in there?" asked Wilmer.

A small voice, so small it could barely be heard, said, "Y-y-yes."

The big cousins looked at one another and ran. They ran back along the path and around the darkening woods. They were snickering and chuckling when they reached Grandma's front porch, where they ate all the candy in the bag they'd promised to Li'l Loudmouth.

They gave Grandma the laundry detergent. "Thank you, my darlin' children," she said. Then she asked, "Where's the littlest one?"

"Oh, he' went upstairs to read a book," lied Wilmer. "We're goin' upstairs, too."

Sunset was about thirty minutes away. Thirty minutes of peace and quiet and no Li'l Loudmouth. But the big trees shaded the yard, and the porch seemed gloomy as they peered at it through the front door screen. The whole house was getting dark, except for the light from the kitchen.

The cousins tiptoed toward the stairs.

"Oooh," said a voice in the shadows at the top of the stairs. *"Oooooh."*

Wilmer, the biggest cousin, stopped and whispered, "What was that?" The voice was low, slow, soft, and menacing. The cousins listened, as the voice moaned again and again, *"Oooh, Oooooh."*

"What is that?" Wilmer asked. He couldn't figure out the sound. It was like a wind blending with a ghostly groan, something he'd never before heard

The other cousins shrugged their shoulders or cringed and shook their heads. They were all too afraid to speak.

"Oooh," said the voice again, *"Oooooh!"*

"Grandma!" Wilmer shouted. "Is there somebody else in the house?"

"Now why would there be somebody else here? Y'all are too noisy for me to have company. And everybody is settling in their own homes for the evening." Grandma spoke from the kitchen.

"*Oooh*," said the voice in the shadows at the top of the stairs.

"Grandma!!!" shouted three of the big cousins at the same time, "Can you come upstairs with us?"

"I'm fixin' your dinner, children," Grandma fussed. "Go on upstairs and play with the littlest one."

Something moved at the top of the stairs. Moved, and growled, and giggled, and seemed to quickly disappear. "GRANDMA!" shouted Wilmer, "Please come here! We're scared!"

But Grandma didn't answer. Grandma didn't say anything. The big cousins walked into the kitchen.

Grandma was gone.

And behind them, coming down the stairs was that voice, "*Oooh*."

The big cousins screamed and cried and ran into one another as, behind them, the back door slammed and feet shuffled. The kitchen light went out. Now, they didn't know which way to turn, for that voice was behind them, and the shuffling in the dark kitchen was coming closer, and closer, and *closer*…

"BOYISCAREDYOUDIDN'TI?" shouted Li'l Loudmouth as he turned on the light in the front hall. "IBETYOUDIDN'TTHINK…"

"Georgie, speak slowly," said Grandma, and she shuffled over to the light over the kitchen sink, turned it on, and said, "Speak slowly, and softer. You have such a loud mouth!"

She and Li'l Loudmouth laughed so hard that Grandma started coughing, and Li'l Loudmouth got the hiccups. But he spoke slowly, and softly, as he told his cousins what he'd done.

"I got scared—hic—in the old Dobbs House. Hic. As soon as I heard you—hic—all running, I ran, too. Hic. But I didn't follow you. Hic. I ran right into the woods—hic—and right into Grandma's back door—hic—and I got here before you—hic—I got here so fast—hic. Because it's a straight line through the woods—hic—not a windy path—hic. And you didn't even know I was here. I told Grandma I thought you were playing tricks on me. Hic. So,

Grandma helped me to play a trick on you—hic. I make good scary noises, don't I? Hic.

"Now—hic." Li'l Loudmouth stepped closer, stood on his tiptoes, raised his arms and shook his hands at his bigger cousins. He growled a low, truly frightening growl, then said, "Where's my...CANDY? OOOOH!"

The cousins all started to talk at the same time, making excuses to Grandma and explanations to the littlest cousin. They sounded like a chorus of Li'l Loudmouths.

"HUSH!" fussed Grandma. "Enough.

"Time for supper. Go wash your sticky hands. And Georgie, you stay with me, drink some water for those hiccups. Then you help me set the table. And after dinner, I've got dessert just for you, homemade strawberry ice cream. Your big cousins already had dessert. I watched them eat that candy. That's why I know they've got sticky fingers. Greedy fingers, too."

The big cousins stared at Georgie. They'd called him Li'l Loudmouth for so long, that they'd almost forgotten his name.

Late that night, the big cousins all huddled together on Georgie's bed. They asked him questions about the straight-line path through the big trees in the woods, and what he'd heard there and what he'd seen, for they'd never had the nerve to go through the woods. Some of them fell asleep on Georgie's bed. Some of them lay whispering on the floor near it, whispering all kinds of questions to Georgie long into the night.

They asked Georgie to teach them how to make those creepy noises... *Oooooh.*

NOTES:

When I was little like Georgie, I sometimes was teased by my bigger cousins. They'd tease me because I laughed too loudly or was too skinny or couldn't easily roller skate or play the very athletic games they played. I'd run to my grandmother and work in the kitchen with her, and I always felt better after a while. And, while the cousins were playing, I helped my grandfather make strawberry ice cream.

The first taste of it always made up for the teasing, since the cousins didn't get any ice cream until after dinner.

In time, I found that there were two things I could do pretty well. I could run faster than most of my cousins, and I could tell very creepy stories. And I did, sometimes about a little boy nicknamed Li'l Loudmouth.

Chapter 2
Things that go "Slurp" in the Night

Bad joke: What do ghosts like for dessert? Boo-berry pie and I scream!

The Pumpkin Tale

By Sherry Norfolk

Baby Boos

In a little old house, there lived a Little Old Woman and Little Old Man. They had a little pumpkin patch out behind the little old house, and it was full of plump orange pumpkins.

"Go fetch me a pumpkin," said the Little Old Woman, "and I'll make us a pumpkin pie."

"Sure thing," answered the Little Old Man with a happy grin. He took a sharp knife and walked slowly out to the pumpkin patch—shuffle-shuffle-shuffle.

He carefully looked at all of the plump orange pumpkins. He chose a perfect little round pumpkin to be made into a pie.

Whack! The Little Old Man cut the tough green stem and carried the little pumpkin back to the Little Old Woman. He set it on the kitchen table.

"Here you go, Darlin'! Want me to help you chop it up?" he asked.

But before the Little Old Woman could answer, that little pumpkin rolled itself off the table! Thump! Then it rolled right out the door! Bumpity-thumpity-thump!

"Come back here!" yelled the Little Old Man, and he chased after the pumpkin—but remember, he was a little OLD man. He couldn't chase very fast. Shuffle-shuffle-shuffle.

The Pumpkin called back,

"Run, walk, roll or fly! `

Can't catch me,

Don't wanna be a pie!"

The pumpkin rolled happily along until it rolled past a Witch, stirring something in a bubbling cauldron. Bloop, bloop, bloop!

"Stop, Little Pumpkin!" called the Witch, "I'll make you into a pie!"

But the Pumpkin called back, "No way! I rolled away from an Old Woman and an Old Man, and I can roll away from you, too!

"Run, walk, roll or fly!

Can't catch me,

Don't wanna be a pie!"

The pumpkin rolled happily along until it rolled past a howling Ghost, "OOOOoooooooOOOOOOoooo!"

"Stop, Little Pumpkin!" moaned the Ghost, "I'll make you into a pie!"

But the Pumpkin called back, "No way! I rolled away from an Old Woman and an Old Man and a Witch, and I can roll away from you, too!

"Run, walk, roll or fly!

Can't catch me,

Don't wanna be a pie!"

The pumpkin rolled happily along until it rolled past a Black Cat, "Meeooooow!"

"Stop, Little Pumpkin!" meowed the Black Cat, "I'll make you into a pie!"

But the Pumpkin called back, "No way! I rolled away from an Old Woman and an Old Man and a Witch and a Ghost, and I can roll away from you, too!

"Run, walk, roll or fly!

Can't catch me,

Don't wanna be a pie!"

The pumpkin rolled happily along until it rolled past a little Bat, "Eee, eee, eee!"

"Stop, Little Pumpkin!" squeaked the little Bat, "I'll make you into a pie!"

But the Pumpkin called back, "No way! I rolled away from an Old Woman and an Old Man and a Witch and a Ghost and a Black Cat, and I can roll away from you, too!

"Run, walk, roll or fly!

Can't catch me,

Don't wanna be a pie!"

The pumpkin rolled happily along until it rolled past a Little Boy, "HEY!"

"Stop, Little Pumpkin!" yelled the Little Boy, "Come back here!"

But the Pumpkin called back, "No way! I rolled away from an Old Woman and an Old Man and a Witch and a Ghost and a Black Cat, and a little Bat, and I can roll away from you, too!

"Run, walk, roll or fly!

Can't catch me,

Don't wanna be a pie!"

But that Little Boy was quick! He grabbed that pumpkin and took it home. Then his dad helped him make that plump orange pumpkin into a plump orange Jack o' Lantern!

The Little Boy stuck a candle inside, and his dad lit it.

And you know what? That plump orange pumpkin was very happy! He didn't want to be a *pie*—but he loved being a jack-o'-lantern!

"Grinning face on Halloween night!
I'm a jack-o'-lantern
What a scary sight!"

NOTES:

This story happily rolls along in the tradition of "The Gingerbread Boy" and all of its variants. Our favorites are *Journeycake, HO!*, an Appalachian version by Ruth Sawyer (Puffin, 1978), Berthe Amoss's *Cajun Gingerbread Boy* (MTC Press, 1999), Anita Lobel's *The Pancake* (Morrow, 1978) and *The Bun: a Tale from Russia* by Marcia Brown (Harcourt Brace Jovanich, 1972).

A cumulative tale provides all sorts of opportunities for participation! The chorus is easily picked up by the listeners, who join in chanting the mocking refrain. This chorus is easy to add actions to, as well, which will engage those kinesthetic kids!

The story is fun to dramatize with kids acting out the various roles or with puppets—emphasizing sequencing, cause-and-effect, and FUN! Yes, fun is important—we want to instill a love of language, reading, books, and stories! We want to motivate story reading and story writing and storytelling. So…we want to have FUN!

Amy and the Crossnore

Adapted by Sherry Norfolk

Baby Boos, Little Boos, and Big Boos

There was once a little girl named Amy, who had a job. That's right—she was no older than you, but she had a job to do, and she did it every single day. Her job was to take her goats up to the top of a high mountain where they could eat the sweet green grass.

Now, Amy loved her goats, and she loved going up the mountain… BUT…but there was one thing she didn't love, and that was the Crossnore! The Crossnore was a monster that lived under the mountain, and Amy knew all about that Crossnore. She knew he wanted to grab her by the toes, pull her down underneath the mountain, and stuff dirt up her nose!

Amy knew all that, but also knew lots more about the Crossnore because she had gone to the library and read every single book she could find about that monster. She knew that he wasn't afraid of guns or bullets. He wasn't afraid of swords or knives. He wasn't afraid of bombs or darkness or spiders or thunder. He wasn't even afraid of karate—hi-yah!

But there was one thing the Crossnore was afraid of, and that was music. When he heard music he would scream, "ARGHHHHHH! I HATE MUSIC! WAAAAAAAHHHHHH!"

Amy knew about that because she had done her homework. So every day when she took her goats up the mountain, she would sing a song to scare the Crossnore:

A-rum-pum-pum	[Pat thighs once, clap 3x in rhythm.]
A-rum-pum-pum	[Pat thighs once, clap 3x in rhythm.]
A-rolly-rolly-rolly-rolly	[Roll hands.]
Rum-pum-pum!	[Pat thighs once, clap 3x in rhythm.]

Down underneath the mountain, the Crossnore would be listening. He would hear Amy's feet go:

Pit-a-pat, pit-a-pat, pit-a-pat. [Pat thighs in rhythm.]

"OH NO, HERE SHE COMES!" he would roar.

He would hear the goats' hooves go:

Trip-trap, trip-trap, trip-trap. [Tap two fingers in your palm rhythmically.]

"OH NO, OH NO—NOW SHE'S GONNA SING THAT SONG!"

And sure, enough, he would hear Amy sing:

A-rum-pum-pum

A-rum-pum-pum

A-rolly-rolly-rolly-rolly

Rum-pum-pum!

"ARGHHHHHH! I HATE MUSIC! WAAAAAAAHHHHHH! ONE OF THESE DAYS, I'M GONNA GRAB THAT KID BY THE TOES, PULL HER DOWN UNDERNEATH THE MOUNTAIN, AND STUFF DIRT UP HER NOSE! HA-HA-HA-HA-HA!"

But he never did, because to get close enough to grab her by the toes and pull her underneath the mountain and stuff dirt up her nose, he would have to get way to close to all that scary music. So Amy was safe…until…

One morning, Amy woke up with a very sore throat. She couldn't talk, much less sing—but she still had to take her goats up the mountain. Amy was scared, but she had a job to do.

She started up the mountain. Her feet went:

Pit-a-pat, pit-a-pat, pit-a-pat.

"OH NO, HERE SHE COMES!" roared the Crossnore.

The goats' hooves went:

Trip-trap, trip-trap, trip- trap.

"OH NO, OH NO—NOW SHE'S GONNA SING THAT SONG!" moaned the Crossnore.

But she didn't sing because her throat was too sore.

"HA-HA-HA-HA-HA! TODAY'S THE DAY! TODAY I'M GONNA GRAB THAT KID BY THE TOES, PULL HER DOWN UNDERNEATH THE MOUNTAIN, AND STUFF DIRT UP HER NOSE! HA-HA-HA-HA-HA!"

And all day long, he got ready. He dug, and he dug, and he dug, and he dug, and he dug, and he dug, and he dug. He dug, and he dug until his big hairy claws were sticking up out of the dirt of the mountain, ready to grab Amy by the toes, pull her underneath the mountain and stuff dirt up her nose!

But all day long, Amy had been thinking. She still couldn't sing, because her throat hurt too much—but there were other ways to make music! Amy looked around the mountaintop. She looked at every branch of every bush and every branch of every tree until she found a long straight hollow branch. Then she took out her pocketknife and very carefully cut that branch off. She poked some holes in it and made herself a flute. And for the rest of the day, she practiced until she could play her song:

La-la-la-la

La-la-la-la

La-la-la-la-la-la-la-la-la

La-la-la

Then she was ready to go back down the mountain.

She started down the mountain. Her feet went:

Pit-a-pat, pit-a-pat, pit-a-pat.

"HA-HA-HA-HA-HA! HERE SHE COMES!" roared the Crossnore.

The goats' hooves went:

Trip-trap, trip-trap, trip- trap.

"HO-HO, HO-HO!" roared the Crossnore. "NOW I'M GONNA GRAB HER BY THE TOES, PULL HER DOWN UNDERNEATH THE MOUNTAIN, AND STUFF DIRT UP HER NOSE! HA-HA-HA-HA-HA!"

But JUST as he was going to grab her by the toes—JUST as he was going to pull her down underneath the mountain and stuff dirt up her nose—Amy pulled out her flute, and she began to play:

La-la-la-la

La-la-la-la

La-la-la-la-la-la-la-la-la

La-la-la

"ARGHHHHHH! I HATE MUSIC! WAAAAAAAHHHHHH!" The Crossnore began to dig.

He dug, and he dug, and he dug, and he dug.

He dug, and he dug, and he dug, and he dug.

He dug, and he dug until he was all the way to the center of the Earth - -as far away as he could get from all that scary music.

You'll never, ever see a Crossnore, because they all live in the very middle of the Earth, as far away as they can get from music.

As for Amy, she still goes up that mountain every day. Her feet still go:

Pit-a-pat, pit-a-pat, pit-a-pat.

The goats' hooves still go:

Trip-trap, trip-trap, trip-trap.

And every day, she still sings her song:

A-rum-pum-pum

A-rum-pum-pum

A-rolly-rolly-rolly-rolly

Rum-pum-pum!

NOTES:

"Amy and the Crossnore" is based on "A Story for Heather" in Nancy Schimmel's *Just Enough to Make a Story* (Sisters' Choice Press, 1978). Nancy graciously gave us permission to include it in ***Boo-Tickle Tales.***

When I tell the story, I use a wooden fife to play Amy's song to scare the Crossnore at the climax of the story. Any song will be fine in that slot— for maximum impact, I chose a song that I can also play on the fife. When the children recognize the song, they say, "Ooooooooh!"

Ahhhhhhh!

This is a story about problem-solving. Amy followed the protocol for solving problems: she identified the problem, thought about possible solutions, evaluated her ideas and chose one, then tried it out. By trying her idea (practicing her flute to make sure it worked), she could predict the probable outcome. If the flute had not made a musical sound, she would have had to re-evaluate her strategy and tried again.

Stories provide opportunities for children to vicariously encounter all sorts of problems and witness how the characters solve them. As the story progresses, listeners and readers are carried along in their imagination. They identify the problem as soon as they learn that Amy can't sing; they begin to worry (empathize) and try to come up with solutions to the problem. When Amy makes the flute, they predict the outcome. Lots of modeling and practicing problem-solving—it's good for the brain! Research tells us that problem solving is one of the brain's favorite exercises.[4] In fact, the brain *only learns* when it is confronted with a problem. So tell 'em stories—problem solved!

The Cupcake Chomper's Mistake

By Lyn Ford

Little Boos and Big Boos

In a town not far from Once-Upon-a-Time lived a herd of monsters. There were big monsters and small monsters, short monsters and tall monsters, Finnywhistlers and Bunderthunkers, Wild haired Greetches and Cupcake Chompers, a Breakfast Blather and her fluffy family, and one Raspberry Fooferboo. All the monsters were wonderfully weird. But the

---

4   Schiller, Pam. *Start Smart: Building Brain Power in the Early Years.* Beltsville, Maryland: Gryphon House, 1999. "Problem-solving and the Brain," 97-104.

Raspberry Fooferboo was the only monster of his kind.

He was shaped like the perfect cupcake freshly pulled from the baking pan. His head was smooth and bald, except for a big, red raspberry bump on the tippy top. That bump perfectly matched the color of the Fooferboo's beady eyes. The little tongue that stuck out of his tiny round mouth. The Fooferboo had no arms or legs; he bounced or rolled wherever he wanted to go, looking very much like a runaway baked good. Each time he bounced, the Fooferboo made a strange little sound: "Eep!" And wherever he rolled, the Fooferboo gave off the scent of raspberries and chocolate chips.

One muggy night, when the moon was hiding from the heat and the air was too warm for sleep, the Fooferboo rolled out of his bed and bounced out the door and through the town in search of a cool place to rest. As he rolled and bounced—"Eep!"—and bounced—"Eep!"—and rolled, the other monsters began to dream of chocolate chip cookies and raspberry jam.

At last, the Fooferboo found a cool and comfy spot in the soft leaves under a pinkle bush next to the lake. The lake was ripply, the pinkles were perfumy, the air was coolly tickling the Fooferboo's raspberry bump. The Fooferboo giggled, wobbled a bit, then sat, "Eep!", and went to sleep.

In the morning, when the Breakfast Blather yelled, "Get up, sloppies! Wash and gargle! Time for morning goodies!", most of the monsters stretched and happily muttered, "Ah, I dreamed of the Fooferboo, the lovely, smelly Fooferboo."

Some yawned and moaned, "Oh, dreamed of chocolate chip pancakes with raspberry syrup for breakfast. Ah, the wonderfully odiferous Fooferboo."

But one Yellow Cupcake Chomper, cried, "Oooh, berries and chocolate, berries and chocolate! Gonna gobble a cupcake today!"

The Yellow Cupcake Chomper snuffled the lingering aroma of Fooferboo, followed it to the edge of the lake, and found the Fooferboo, still asleep under the pinkle bush.

The Yellow Cupcake Chomper drooled and grinned. "Ooh, aah, cupcake," he said, just before he swallowed the Fooferboo in one ghoulish

"GULP."

"Eep!" cried the Fooferboo in the Cupcake Chomper's belly. But the Cupcake Chomper just grinned and wiped his slobbery lips.

He walked back to town, and to the town square, where the Breakfast Blather had set the tables and the monsters' breakfasts were ready. There were big meals for the big monsters, small meals for the small monsters, long loaves of bread for the tall monsters, and shortbread for the short monsters. There were french fries for the Finnywhistlers, bagels for the Bunderthunkers, waffles for the Wild haired Greetches, cupcakes for the Cupcake Chompers, and one fat, red raspberry for the Raspberry Fooferboo.

As usual, breakfast was a riot of gobbles and munches and snorts and chokes and burps. All the monsters chomped and chewed.

But no one said, "Eep!", for the Fooferboo was missing.

The Breakfast Blather, nibbling on a blueberry muffin, squawked, "Stop chomping, sloppies! Where's the Fooferboo?"

Monsters looked around, under the table, beneath the benches, in their pajama pockets, all, that is, except the Yellow Cupcake Chomper. He sat very still. He didn't say a word. But his stomach did. It said, "Eep!"

The Breakfast Blather stared at that Cupcake Chomper's belly. "Cupcake sloppy," said the Breakfast Blather, "your tummy is talking. What did it say?"

"Um," said the Yellow Cupcake Chomper, "it said, 'Good morning, and thank you for the delicious cupcake.'"

"Eep!" said his stomach.

"That didn't sound like a good morning or a thank-you," grumbled the Breakfast Blather. "That sounded like an 'eep.'

"Why would your tummy say, 'eep'?"

"Um," said the Yellow Cupcake Chomper, "maybe, it's hungry."

"Eep!" said his stomach.

The other monsters stared at that Cupcake Chomper's belly.

"Well," said a Green Cupcake Chomper, "if your tummy is hungry, why don't you eat your cupcake?"

"Um," the Yellow Cupcake Chomper said, "maybe, it's not hungry. Maybe, it's tired."

"Eep!" said his stomach.

"Balderdash!" fussed a huge Bunderthunker. "A tired belly would snore, not 'eep.' That was definitely an 'eep' coming from behind your belly button. Why does your stomach say, 'eep?'" The Bunderthunker frowned and glared at the Cupcake Chomper.

"Um, uh, well…" the yellow Cupcake Chomper stammered, "m-m-maybe, it's sick?"

"Eep!" said his stomach.

The Breakfast Blather shook her feathers, "Ridiculous. Absolutely ridiculous. That is not a sick-belly sound, sloppy. That is the cry of a Raspberry Fooferboo!"

The Breakfast Blather grabbed the Yellow Cupcake Chomper with her mighty claws. She shook him and screeched, "You greedy guts! You nasty noodle! You selfish sloppy! You have gobbled our one and only Raspberry Fooferboo!" With each shake, the Yellow Cupcake Chomper's belly said, "Eep!"

The Yellow Cupcake Chomper pulled himself away from the Breakfast Blather. But the other monsters caught him and pushed him to the ground. The Breakfast Blather jumped up and down and up and down on his belly as she shouted, "Sloppy! Sloppy! Greedy and gobbly!" With each jump, a tiny voice squealed, "Eep!"

Then, suddenly, BOING! The Raspberry Fooferboo popped out of the Yellow Cupcake Chomper's mouth. It bounced, "Eep! Eep! EEP!" and landed on the breakfast table, where it quickly swallowed the one fat, red raspberry.

"Eep!" said the Raspberry Fooferboo with a smile.

"Sorry," whimpered the Yellow Cupcake Chomper.

"No worries, sloppy," said the Breakfast Blather. "Happens every morning after a muggy night."

The monsters went back to mangling their breakfast. And all was as it should be in a town full of monsters not far from Once-Upon-a-Time.

NOTES:

This is a kinder, gentler spin on an absolutely horrific folktale, whose motif is known as "Mother killed me, Father ate me." Gruesome! And yet… what story from the collections of the Brothers Grimm *isn't* gruesome???

The tale that prompted my retelling can be found in *Children's and Household Tales—Grimms' Fairy Tales, or Kinder- und Hausmärchen No. 47.* There are variants from Austria, England, Romania, Scotland, and my own beloved multicultural African American Appalachia, which for my family and me is Affrilachia. But the variant I've created is from the heart of a grandma who fears deliberately scaring her grandbabies.

As long as they feel safe, kids love things that go slurp and chomp in the night. And as long as there's a safe and satisfying ending, they're okay with monsters gobbling and burping up other creatures. In my story, the gobbler apologizes, the gobbled creature happily eats its breakfast, all is forgiven, and life goes on.

For another gobbling-critter story with a happy ending, see "The Thing in the Woods I."

The Thing in the Woods I

By Lyn Ford

Little Boos and Big Boos

Once there was a boy named Ayo. He lived in a small village with his father, his mother, his sister, his brother, and his great-auntie. One day, his father and big brother gave him a little drum. His father placed the carrying strap of the drum over Ayo's shoulder and patted him on the head. His brother said, "Practice every day, little brother, and one day you will be able to play with us at any village gathering or celebration."

Every day, when his chores were done, Ayo practiced on his drum. He played *slooowly slooowly*, and quickly, quickly quickly. Ayo played LOUDLY LOUDLY, and softly…softly…softly.

And every day, Ayo's father and mother and sister and brother praised him for the way he practiced faithfully. But Ayo's auntie always said, "Stop playing that drum!"

You see, Auntie had a sore tooth in her head. And every time Ayo hit the drum, Auntie could feel it in her tooth. He'd hit the drum *pum*. Auntie would grab her jaw and say, "Ow!" Ayo hit the drum *pampampam*. Auntie shouted, "OwOwOw!"

And, finally, Auntie yelled, "Ayo, stop playing that drum!" But on this day, she also made a suggestion.

"Ayo," she said, "Take one of my baskets and go down into the deepest, darkest part of the woods, where the biggest, sweetest berries grow. Pick some of those berries, fill the basket, bring it back, and I will make something good for you.

"And when you go down into the woods, don't leave that drum here where somebody might hit it—I mean, *play it.* Take that drum with you."

Auntie tried to give Ayo a big, big basket to fill. In that way, he wouldn't be playing his drum for a long time. And if he did play it, he would be in the deepest, darkest part of the forest. Auntie wouldn't hear the drum.

But Ayo shook his head and held tightly to the drum strap. "Auntie, I don't want to pick berries in the deepest, darkest part of the woods," he said. "My friend went down there just the other day, and he said there's a strange thing in the woods. My friend said the strange thing lives in the bushes, and it tried to eat him!"

"Nonsense," said Auntie. "Your friend was just trying to scare you. Take this basket. GO pick the berries. And take that drum with you!"

Ayo said, "Yes, ma'am. He put the basket over his shoulder. And all the way down into the deepest, darkest part of the woods, Ayo played his drum. He played *slooowly slooowly,* and quickly, quickly quickly. He played LOUDLY LOUDLY, and softly…softly…softly.

And in no time at all, Ayo was in the deepest, darkest part of the woods. A little sunlight made its way through the thick canopy of leaves. Ayo could see the bushes, on which grew berries as big as his head!

Ayo took the basket from his shoulder and set it on the ground. He removed the drum strap from his other shoulder and set his drum next to the basket. He picked the berries, which were so big that three would fill the basket.

Ayo pulled three berries from the bushes, one, two, three.

Suddenly, he heard a rustling sound in the bushes. Then Ayo saw two big, googly eyeballs peering at him through the bushes. Then something huge and hairy leaped from the bushes, waved its long arms above its monstrous head, and yelled at Ayo, "Googly oogy yaga oo!"

Ayo asked, "W-what?"

The thing waved its arms again and said, "Googly oogy yaga oo!"

Ayo said, "I-I'm s-sorry. I didn't understand a word you said."

The thing put his furry hands on his hips and shook his head. Then he repeated, "Googly"—and he pointed to himself—"oogy"—and he pointed at Ayo—"yaga"—and he opened his mouth and pointed inside—"oo"—and he pointed at Ayo again.

"Oh," said Ayo, "You're…gonna…eat me?"

The thing rubbed his belly and grinned and shook his horrible head, "Mmmmm."

Ayo was so nervous that he snatched up his drum. His trembling fingers tapped against the drum head.

The thing curiously looked at the drum and questioned, "Oomp?"

Ayo asked, "Do you like that sound?"

The thing said, "Oomp!"

Would you like to hear more of that sound?" asked Ayo.

The thing said, "Ooomp!"

Ayo took a deep breath and played his drum. He played *slooowly slooowly*, and quickly, quickly quickly. He played LOUDLY LOUDLY, and softly…softly…softly.

The thing rocked back and forth and twirled around and around. The thing was dancing!

Ayo played faster. The thing twirled faster. Ayo played faster! The thing twirled faster! Ayo played faster and faster and faster and faster, and the thing twirled faster and faster and faster in its dance.

Then it stopped, and held its head. The thing said, "Oooh."

It grabbed its belly and shook its head. The thing said, "Ooooooh."

Then the thing said, "Urp," covered its mouth, and ran into the bushes.

And Ayo, still tightly holding his drum, ran all the way home.

When he got there, his father and his mother and his sister and his brother hugged him tightly. "Where were you?" Each of them asked. But his Auntie only held her jaw and asked, "Where's my basket?

"Down in the deep dark woods, where you sent me to pick those big berries, Auntie," whimpered Ayo. "And you were wrong! My friend was right! There *is* a strange thing in the woods! It tried to *eat me!*"

Ayo's family tried to comfort him. "Oh, Ayo, if we'd known that

Auntie wanted you to bring berries from the deepest, darkest part of the woods, we would have gone with you to pick them!

"Let's all go back there now. There's no strange thing in the woods. We'll get your auntie's basket. We'll each take a basket, too, and pick a lot of berries!"

Each member of the family found a basket and started walking into the woods. Ayo followed them, but he carried his drum. And when Auntie saw that everyone was walking into the woods, she grabbed a basket herself, and she followed the rest of her family into the woods.

As they walked, Ayo played his drum. How did he play? Yes, you remember! He played *slooowly slooowly*, and quickly, quickly quickly. He played LOUDLY LOUDLY, and softly…softly…softly.

As they walked, Auntie yelled, "Stop playing *that drum!*"

In no time at all, the family was in the deepest, darkest part of the woods. A little sunlight made its way through the thick canopy of leaves. They could see the bushes, on which grew berries as big as their heads!

They sat down their baskets. Ayo sat down his drum so that he could help everyone.

Each of them pulled three berries from the bushes, one, two, three.

Suddenly, they heard a rustling sound in the bushes. Then they saw two big, googly eyeballs peering at them through the bushes. Then something huge and hairy leaped from the bushes, waved its long arms above its monstrous head, and yelled at them, "Googly oogy yaga oo!"

The family asked, "W-what?"

The thing waved its arms again and said, "Googly oogy yaga oo!"

The family said, "We're s-sorry. We didn't understand a word you said."

The thing put his furry hands on his hips and shook his head. Then he repeated, "Googly"—and he pointed to himself—"oogy"—and he pointed at the family—"yaga"—and he opened his mouth and pointed inside—"oo"—and he pointed at the family again.

"Oh," said everyone in the family, "You're…gonna…eat us?"

The thing rubbed his belly and grinned and shook his horrible head, "Mmmmm."

But Ayo remembered what had happened the last time he was in the deepest, darkest part of the woods. He reached for his drum, ready to play and make the thing dance. But his drum was gone!

Auntie had hung the drum by its strap in a little tree so that Ayo wouldn't play while the family picked berries. Ayo stretched his hands toward it, but it was just out of his reach!

The thing walked toward Father and Mother. They were too afraid to move. The thing opened its mouth, wide, wider, wider, and swallowed Father and Mother in one big GULP!

Ayo stood on tiptoes and tried to grab his drum.

The thing walked toward Sister and Brother. They were too afraid to move. The thing opened its mouth, wide, wider, wider, and swallowed Sister and Brother in one big GULP!

Ayo jumped and jumped and pulled at the strap on his drum.

The thing walked toward Auntie. She was too afraid to move. The thing opened its mouth, wide, wider, wider, and, just as Ayo yanked his drum from the branch of the little tree, the thing swallowed Auntie in one big GULP!

Then the thing turned toward Ayo.

"Wait a minute!" Ayo shouted. He patted his drum. He asked the thing, "Do you remember this?"

The thing looked at the drum and grinned, "Oomp!"

"Would you like to hear it again?" asked Ayo.

The thing shook his head, "Oomp!"

And Ayo began to play. He played *slooowly slooowly*, and quickly, quickly quickly. He played LOUDLY LOUDLY, and softly…softly…softly. He played *slooowly slooowly*, and quickly, quickly quickly. He played LOUDLY LOUDLY, and softly…softly…softly.

Ayo played, and the thing danced and twirled, faster and faster and faster and faster and faster and faster and faster, then…

It stopped, and held its head. The thing said, "Oooh."

It grabbed its belly and shook its head. The thing said, "Ooooooh."

Then the thing said, "Uuuurp," and spit out Father and Mother.

Ayo played again, faster and faster and faster and faster and faster. The thing danced and twirled, faster and faster and faster and faster and faster, and then…

It stopped, and held its head. The thing said, "Oooh."

It grabbed its belly and shook its head. The thing said, "Ooooooh."

Then the thing said, "Uuuurp," and spit out Sister and Brother.

Then, Ayo stopped playing his drum.

His family said, "Oh, thank you, Ayo, for saving us from that horrible thing. But, where is your auntie?"

Ayo sheepishly grinned and said, "She's inside the strange thing."

"Oh, no!" cried his family, "Get her out of there!" Ayo frowned, "Do I have to?"

His father said, "Yes, you do."

His mother said, "She is family."

His Sister said, "And even when we are upset with one another, we help one another."

His Brother said, "Now, hurry up, and get your great-auntie out of that creature!"

Ayo shrugged. He played his drum. How? *Slooowly slooowly*, and quickly, quickly quickly. He played LOUDLY LOUDLY, and softly…softly… softly, and faster and faster and faster and faster and faster, and the thing twirled faster and faster and faster and faster and faster, and then…

Yep.

The thing stopped, and held its head. The thing said, "Oooh."

It grabbed its belly and shook its head. The thing said, "Ooooooh."

Then the thing said, "Uuuurp," and spit out Auntie.

Then that thing ran into the bushes. And Ayo and his family ran with the baskets and the drum. They ran until they were all safe at home.

As Ayo's father and his mother and his sister and his brother talked about the strange thing they'd met, and the strange adventure they'd had, they noticed that Auntie was smiling. She hadn't smiled in a long time.

Auntie hugged Ayo and said to him, "You keep practicing on that drum, sweet boy. You practice as much and as long as you like!"

And she meant it! She didn't mind the sound of Ayo's drum anymore. You see, somewhere in their adventure, that tooth that had troubled Auntie had fallen right out of her mouth. It didn't hurt anymore when Ayo played his drum. But even if it had, she would've wanted him to play.

And what happened to that thing? Well, it seems that it kept a belly ache, as if something as small and as sharp as a tooth was poking just behind its belly button. The thing decided that people weren't good to eat. It disappeared and was never, ever seen again.

NOTE:

Ayo is a boy's name from the Yoruba culture of West Africa; the name means "joy." I heard the story as an Affrilachian folktale, and the berries were berries. When I tell the story, the boy has no name; in my family, many tales were told with protagonists called "Little Girl, "Little Boy," "Auntie," etc. But I've been told that the roots of this story are West African, and, in the story as printed format, I felt the boy needed a name.

When I tell the story, young participants get to be the voice of the thing as he explains his meal plans to the family. The sounds they create are hilarious! I let them do the burping "uuurp," sounds, too. A good belch always adds something to a monstrous tale.

There are a lot of sounds to play with in this one, and a lot of actions. It's fun to play Ayo's drumbeats on a small *djembe* or bongo. But if you don't have a drum available, pat on your legs or clap your hands to the rhythms of Ayo's drum.

Now I've Got Ya!

By Sherry Norfolk

Big Boos

Have you ever looked in a mirror and—just for a second—seen the reflection of someone else close beside you? Someone who isn't there?

Have you ever walked down a street alone and heard the sound of someone else's footsteps following along behind?

Have you ever felt a creepy, tickly touch on the back of your neck when no one else is around?

Things like that happened to Adam every day.

Every.

Day.

And they happened every night.

Every.

Night.

Doorknobs rattled and shook when no one was on the other side.

Cold drafts wafted across his neck when there were no windows open.

And no one else ever saw or heard or felt them. No one ever believed Adam. No one.

"Did you see that?" he would demand, looking wildly around. "Shhh! Did you hear that? Did you feel that?" But people would just shake their heads and look away. Sometimes they laughed at him and called him names. But most of the time, they simply ignored him.

But Adam knew that *something* was there…something was always there…just out of reach…just out of sight…waiting, waiting, waiting…

One dark midnight, Adam woke up to a scratching, scraping sound by the window. *Scraaaatttch…scraaaaattch…*He stretched his eyes wide and strained to see what was on the other side of that glass. The curtain moved…

"AAAAAAAAAAAH!" Adam screamed, and for the thousandth time, his father came running to his room in the middle of the night.

"There's nothing THERE," his father repeated over and over again when Adam told him what he had heard and seen.

"But I *saw* it—right over there, something crawling in the window! It was *there*, Dad, it *was*!" Adam held the covers up close to his chin.

His father sat down on the edge of the bed, and for the thousandth time, he explained, "Son, you just have a vivid imagination. There's nothing THERE. Nothing is going to get you. You have to get over this, Adam!"

But Adam knew. He knew that something was there.

One evening, Adam's mom and dad announced that they were going to a birthday party and that Adam would be staying home alone.

"Don't worry, Son, you're going to be fine," Dad assured him quickly as a look of panic spread across Adam's face. "You're 12 years old—plenty old enough to stay home alone for a couple of hours—and we'll be back before dark. We'll lock up tight, and we'll have our cell phones with us—but you won't need to call us because nothing will happen. Just relax and watch TV after you finish your homework."

Adam swallowed hard and nodded his head. He knew there was no use in arguing—and besides, he couldn't get any words out past the knot in his stomach and the lump in his throat.

"Alright, Adam, we've locked all the windows and drawn the curtains, and we've locked all the doors. You'll be snug as a bug in a rug! Now just do your homework and watch TV and we'll be home before you know it," Mom said, and she gave him a little kiss and warm hug. "You'll be just fine."

After they had left, Adam turned on every light in the house and double-checked all the locks on all the doors and windows. He did NOT do his homework—his hands were shaking too badly to write. He did NOT turn on the TV—he didn't want its noise to mask any sounds that might be made.

What did he do? He walked, slowly and silently through empty rooms, waiting and listening, waiting and watching, waiting…waiting…waiting…

And then he heard it. A soft, sinister voice, off-key and haunting, "Now I've got you…where I want you…now I'm going to EAT you!"

"What's that?" Adam froze and listened, trying to figure out where the voice was coming from.

"Now I've got you…where I want you…now I'm going to EAT you!"

From upstairs? From the basement? From all over the house…the voice seemed to come from everywhere and nowhere at once…

"Now I've got you…where I want you…now I'm going to EAT you!"

Adam raced from room to room, listening, following, moving furniture, checking under beds and inside closets and behind shower curtains…

"Now I've got you…where I want you…now I'm going to EAT you!"

And there it was: hairy and grinning and swinging from the rafters of the garage…

"Now I've got you…where I want you…now I'm going to EAT you!"

The little monkey swung down to the floor, broke a banana off of a bunch that lay there, and peeled it as he sang, "Now I've got you…where I want you…now I'm going to EAT you!"

The monkey took a big bite of the banana and grinned up at Adam.

Adam took the monkey into the house and played with him until his parents came home.

"Alright, you got me!" he said. "I guess you taught me a lesson tonight. Thanks—I think."

"We just wanted you to have a new pet," smiled Mom, "and we wanted it to be a surprise."

"It was a surprise, alright," said Adam. And with his new pet keeping him company, Adam was never alone again.

NOTES

"Now I've Got Ya" is one of those campfire tales that have been told to kids gathered in the darkness around a smoking fire for decades. They are heard and passed on in the folk tradition. They are almost always sort of—but not quite—scary.

The first time I heard "Now I've Got Ya" was in an entirely different setting, at The National Storytelling Festival in Jonesborough, Tennessee. Under the iconic striped tent, surrounded by hundreds of adults, I heard Ed Stivender tell that story, with a bit of a twist at the end: "And there sat a little monkey, picking boogers out of his nose. He stuck a booger in his mouth and sang, 'Now I've got ya, where I want ya, now I'm gonna eat ya!' Slurp! Pure Ed Stivender!

I've found that telling this story directly after one like "The Hairy Toe" increases the impact. The audience expects another jump story and willingly suspends disbelief, allowing you to string them along to the very end!

An excellent resource for more campfire stories is found on *American Folklore* website's "Spooky Campfire Stories" page at http://www.american-folklore.net/campfire.html

CHAPTER 3
BOOS AND BONES AND GRAVEYARD STONES

Bad joke: Why is a cemetery a great place to write
a story? Because it has so many plots!

Billy Brown and the Belly Button Monster

Adapted by Bobby and Sherry Norfolk

Little Boos and Big Boos

Once there was a boy named Billy Brown. Billy Brown had chocolate brown skin. He had curly black hair. He had big brown eyes, and he had a round brown belly. And right in the middle of his round brown belly, he had a perfectly round, brown belly button.

Every night, Billy Brown's mama tucked him in bed, and every night she said, "Now don't you go kicking those covers off tonight, Billy Brown, or you'll catch a cold!"

Every night, Billy Brown sighed, "Oh, Mo-o-om! Phooey!" Then his mama kissed him goodnight—smack—she turned off the light—click!—and

Billy Brown twisted, and he turned, and he flipped, and he flopped and Fwump! He kicked off the covers.

One cold night, Billy Brown's mama said, "Don't you go kicking those covers off tonight, Billy Brown, or you'll catch pneumonia!"

Billy Brown sighed, "Oh, Mo-o-om! Phooey!" Then his mama kissed him goodnight—smack! She turned off the light—click—and Billy Brown twisted, and he turned, and he flipped, and he flopped and Fwump! He kicked off the covers.

The very next night, Billy Brown's mama said, "Don't you go kicking those covers off tonight, Billy Brown. Because if you do, the Belly Button Monster is gonna come and take your belly button right...out...of the middle...of your...BELLY!"

Billy Brown sighed, "Oh, Mo-o-om! Phooey! You can't scare me like that! I know there's no such thing as a Belly Button Monster!"

His mama said, "I wouldn't go trying to find out if I were YOU, Billy Brown. " She kissed him goodnight—smack! She turned off the light—click! Then Billy Brown called after her, "I'm not scared of any Belly Button Monster! I don't believe in a Belly Button Monster, 'cause there's no such thing…I hope!"

Billy Brown decided to keep those covers right up under his chin that night. He held on tight, and he did not move, until just before he fell asleep. And then he began to twist. And turn. And flip. And flop and fwump! He kicked off the covers and went to sleep.

He was so sound asleep, he did not know when the Belly Button Monster appeared at the foot of his bed.

Fwump! He did not see the Belly Button Monster's face, with its two squinty belly button eyes, and its drippy belly button nose, and its slobbery belly button mouth and its floppy belly button ears. He did not see the Belly Button Monster's bag, or hear him sing in a creaky, screechy voice,

"I'm the Belly Button Monster,

I have a Belly Button Bag.

If I see your belly button,

Your belly button I will snag."

He certainly did not see the Belly Button Monster's finger begin to grow longer, and longer, and lo-o-nger and lo-o-o-nger until—SCRONK! It took Billy Brown's belly button right out of the middle of his belly!

"Wow!" gloated the Belly Button Monster, "This really IS a perfectly round brown belly button! It's the very best belly button in the whole belly button bag!"

The Belly Button Monster plopped Billy Brown's belly button into the belly button bag and—Thwump! He disappeared.

Billy Brown stayed sound asleep until morning. When he woke up, he felt perfectly normal, so he went down to the kitchen and picked up the glass of milk that his mama always left for him, and he drank it.

Then all of a sudden, Billy Brown heard a funny sound, like, "Bloop, bloop, bloop!" And he felt something cold and wet trickling down his belly. He looked down...the milk he had just drunk was coming out a hole in the middle of his belly! Bloop, bloop, bloop!

"Oh no! There really is a Belly Button Monster! It got my belly button! What am I gonna do?" Billy Brown began to run around the kitchen clutching his belly, trying to keep the milk from running out the hole. Then he stopped.

"I've gotta be quiet, or Mom'll say, 'I told you so, Billy Brown!' What am I gonna do?" Billy Brown stood still for a moment and thought.

"I know! I'll take a bath. If I clean up all the milk, she'll never know!"

So Billy Brown went upstairs and made a big bubble bath and climbed in.

"Ah-h-h-h!"

But just as he closed his eyes and began to relax, he heard, "Bloop, bloop, bloop!" He looked down—all the bubbles were pouring right into the hole in the middle of his belly! Bloop-bloop-bloop-bloop-bloop-bloop-bloop! His belly was getting bigger, and bigger and bigger!

"Oh, man, I can't go to school like this! I've gotta get rid of all these bubbles!"

Billy Brown began to squeeze his belly—Bloop-bloop-bloop-bloop-bloop-bloop-bloop!—until all the bubbles were out of his belly and filling up the bathroom.

It took every single towel in the house to clean up the mess, but Billy Brown finally got dressed and went to school.

When Billy Brown got to school, his friends stared at him. "Hey, Billy Brown, you look SICK!"

"Wait'll you see THIS!" said Billy Brown, and he raised up his tee-shirt.

"Hey, Billy Brown, your belly button is missing! There's a hole in the middle of your belly! There really IS a Belly Button Monster! He got your belly button, Billy Brown! What're you gonna DO?"

"I don't know," moaned Billy Brown, "I think I'm gonna DIE! Every time I drink or eat anything, it comes right out the hole. And if I sit in water, it pours right in. Yep, I think I'm gonna DIE!"

"You don't have to die, Billy Brown," said his best friend. "All we have to do is figure out a way to stop up the hole in the middle of your belly!"

So all the boys filed into the boys' bathroom and began to pull stuff out of their pockets and try it out in Billy Brown's belly. They tried bubblegum and candy and string and tape. They tried frogs and worms and bugs. They tried a whistle and the key to somebody's house. Nothing worked. As soon as Billy Brown took a sip of water, the plug would pop out, and Billy Brown would be belly-buttonless once more.

"It's never gonna work! I'm just gonna die!" groaned Billy Brown.

"Wait a minute, don't give up," his best friend said. "I've been holding out of on you, Billy Brown. Here, try this." He reached into his pocket and pulled out a small milk chocolate candy bar. He held it out to Billy Brown.

Billy Brown took the chocolate and looked at it sadly.

"It's no use," he said. "I've tried other kinds of candy and nothing worked." He stood staring at the chocolate—then his face lit up.

"Wait a minute! I can't stop up the hole in the middle of my belly with this, but maybe I can use it to trick the Belly Button Monster into giving me back my own round, brown belly button!"

Billy Brown unwrapped the chocolate. It was exactly the color of his own chocolate brown skin. Then he used his thumb to round the piece of chocolate until it was perfectly round and brown—exactly like his own round brown belly button!

"Now let's see how it looks." He put the chocolate into the hole. It looked exactly like his own round brown belly button—but it smelled a whole lot better.

Billy Brown went home, got into bed and pulled the covers up to his chin. Then he began to twist and turn and flip and flop—but just before he kicked off the covers he called out, "I sure do hope the Belly Button Monster doesn't know I have a new, even better, round brown belly button!" Then Fwump! He kicked off the covers and pretended to go to sleep.

And he watched...but nothing happened. So he flipped...and nothing happened. So he flopped...Thwump! There stood the Belly Button Monster.

Sniff! Sniff-sniff! *"Hey!* That is an even better round brown belly button!"

I'm the Belly Button Monster,

I have a Belly Button Bag.

If I see your belly button,

Your belly button I will snag."

The Belly Button Monster's finger begin to grow longer, and longer, and lo-o-nger and lo-o-o-nger until—just before it reached Billy Brown's new round brown belly button—Billy Brown sat up in bed and shouted, *"Boo!"*

The Belly Button Monster screamed and began to shiver and shake. "You scared me! Why'd you go and do a thing like that?"

"I want my own round brown belly button back, that's why!" retorted Billy Brown.

"No-o-o-o! I never ever, ever give back belly buttons, but…*Sniff!* Sniff-sniff!…That sure does smell good! Gimmee, gimmee, gimmee!"

"No!" yelled Billy Brown. "But I'll trade you. You can have this belly button if you'll give my old belly button back."

The Belly Button Monster thought, and sniffed some more, and thought some more.

"No!" he decided. "But I'll make a deal. If you can find your belly button in the belly button bag, you can have it back. But if you can't, I get both of them!"

"Deal!" shouted Billy Brown.

The Belly Button Monster opened up the belly button bag, and Billy Brown looked in. Oh, man! There were *thousands* of belly buttons in the belly button bag! There were hairy ones, and slimy ones, and stinky ones, and fuzzy ones. There were all different shapes and sizes and colors. Billy Brown was just about to give up when, *"Got it!"* He pulled a perfectly round brown belly button out of the belly button bag.

"Now I have to make sure it still works," he said. He took out the piece of chocolate and put his own round brown belly button in place. Then he picked up a glass of water and drank. Nothing happened!

"It works!" shouted Billy Brown. "Here ya go!"

The Belly Button Monster took the piece of chocolate. *Sniff!* Sniff-sniff! Gobble-gobble-gobble-gobble-gobble! And he disappeared. Thwump!

Ever since that night, the Belly Button Monster has never stolen another belly button. But if you have an extra piece of milk chocolate lying around—you better watch out!

NOTES:

Inspired by and loosely based on a Japanese folktale, this story was originally published as a picture book titled *Billy Brown and the Belly Button Beastie* by Bobby and Sherry Norfolk; reprinted with permission from August House LittleFolk, 2007.

Other versions of the story include Judy Sierra's Tasty *Baby Belly Buttons* (Knopf Books for Young Readers; 1st edition, 1999). According to legend, Japanese villagers once lived in fear of great hulking ogres called Onis who considered babies' belly buttons the tastiest of all treats. When they raided a village it was the babies they stole; and, "The Bellybutton Monster" by Olga Loya in *More Ready-to-Tell-Tales from Around the World* (August House, 2000) by David Holt and Bill Mooney.

"The Belly Button Monster" is tons of fun to tell. And it has a wonderful message about what happens when you disobey your parents, and you're disrespectful. Don't be surprised if you see kids covering their belly buttons!

Billy Brown turns out to be a non-violent problem-solver, just like Amy in "Amy and the Crossnore" and Li'l Loudmouth. They all could have theoretically solved their problems with fists or guns or bombs (unfortunately, these "solutions" seem to be popular methods of solving problems in our society), but instead, they chose brain over brawn to get the job done.

Billy has trouble identifying the problem, at first thinking that he simply needs to stop up the hole in the middle of his belly. But when he realizes that his real problem is retrieving his own round, brown belly button, he quickly strategizes and succeeds!

Kids need to recognize that they, too, can be non-violent problem-solvers. Like Billy, they may cause their own problems—and like Billy, their attempts to solve their problems may not always work. But if they learn from their failures, search for alternative solutions, and keep on trying, they are very likely to succeed!

"Turn Me Over!"

Retold by Sherry Norfolk

Big Boos

There once was an old woman who lived right at the edge of the graveyard. Now, most people wouldn't like living by a graveyard, but she didn't mind. She'd lived there all of her life, and she had known everyone that was buried there.

The old woman had outlived all of her friends and relatives, so every evening, just at dark-thirty, she would take a walk through the graveyard, stopping to visit at the graves of her friends and telling them all about her day.

One evening as she was walking down the path between the graves, she heard a high, thin voice. It seemed to be coming from one of the graves:

Tuuuuuuurn me ooooooooooooverrrr!

The old woman gasped and stopped, listening hard and peering around in the gloom.

Tuuuuuuurn me oooooooooooverrrr!

With a little shriek, she began to hurry home just as fast as she could—which wasn't very fast because she was very old and the path was rough and bumpy. Her knees shook, and her tottering steps faltered…

Tuuuuuuurn me oooooooooooverrrr!

She stopped again and muttered to herself.

"Well now, what am I afraid of? I know ever'one who's buried in this here cemetery, and none of 'em would do me no harm. Besides, whoever—or whatever—it seems to need some help, and maybe I'm just the one to give it."

And with that decision firmly made, the old woman began to listen for the voice, following it in and out among the graves, around the tombstones, until she came to the place where the voice was the loudest.

Tuuuuuuurn me oooooooooooverrrr!

It was a tomb, the kind with gargoyles frowning from the corners and tiny dark windows for the souls of the dead to look out. The old woman hesitated there, her old eyes squinting and searching the gathering darkness…those stony gargoyle eyes seemed to be watching her…she felt the presence of something else watching from inside…

Tuuuuuuurn me oooooooooooverrrr!

The old woman stumbled on, slowly circling the tomb…and saw, to her surprise, that the door of the tomb was slightly ajar…so she slowly reached out and pushed it further open…CREEEEEEEEEEAAAAK!

"Eeek!" she squeaked.

Something white and wispy moved inside the tomb, and a horrible smell came rolling out. But in the furthest corner, there was a golden glow. It was from that glow that the voice was emanating, growing louder and louder.

TUUUUUUURN ME OOOOOOOOOOOVERRRR!

Cautiously, the old woman took a tiny step inside the tomb. She took another step, and another, until finally, she stood before the source of that glow…

It was a barbecue grill.

And on top of the grill, there was a hamburger, burnt on the bottom and raw on the top. The hamburger begged,

TUUUUUUURN ME OOOOOOOOOOOVERRRR!

So the old woman looked around and found a spatula, and she flipped that hamburger over.

And the hamburger said, "Thank you!"

NOTES:

Source: "The Graveyard Voice" by Betty Lehrman in *Scared Witless: Thirteen Eerie Tales to Tell* by Martha Hamilton and Mitch Weiss. (August House, 2006.) Betty Lehrman's version is also found in *The Ghost & I: Scary Story for Participatory Telling* edited by Jennifer Justice (Yellow Moon Press, 1992).

Betty says it's a traditional tale that has been passed along by word of mouth for decades. In her participatory version of the story, the protagonist is a family man. Others tell it with a little girl or a couple of boys—but the ending is always the same!

This is not a story for little kids, who often don't get the joke and simply retain the terrifying image of walking through a darkening graveyard and hearing weird voices. But kids who get it will always want to retell this tale, and should be encouraged to do so as long as they don't tell it to their younger siblings!

Like all "scary" stories, it's important to tell "Turn Me Over" with total commitment—if the teller gets a gleeful look on his face or a giggle in her voice, it's all over! Sherry likes to use it at the end of a ghost program, letting the audience leave with a smile on their faces, or as a change-of-pace between a ghost story and a different kind of tale.

The Thing in the Woods II

By Lyn Ford

Little Boos and Big Boos

Once upon a time, about time and a half ago, an old woman went into the woods to look for flowers to pretty her table and blackberries to fill her belly. She had filled a small basket with flowers, and her apron pocket with berries. But her apron had two pockets, and her dress had four long pockets, so she thought she'd go deeper into the woods and find something else that was pretty for the table, or something else that was sweet and good to eat.

Instead, she found a big hairy thing with a runny nose, floppy ears, and very stinky feet.

"Snort," snorted the thing. "Old woman, you are stealing my flowers. If you don't pay me something for them, I'm going to gobble you up." The thing sniffed and snorted again, and wiped its nose on the back of its hairy hand.

"Hmpf," said the old woman, "I don't see how you could own these flowers. But if you do, I'll pay you something for them. How about some of these fine blackberries?"

"Snort," snorted the thing. "Those blackberries belong to my daddy. You'll have to pay him, too." He sniffed and snorted and wiped his nose again.

"Oh, bother," said the old woman. "Well, how about you taking my handkerchief for your nose. That's payment, and you *need* a handkerchief. And how about me giving your daddy my apron to pay for the blackberries?"

The old woman poured the berries she'd gathered in her apron pockets into the basket of flowers. Then she set down the basket and removed her apron. She folded it neatly, then reached into one of the many pockets on her long dress; she pulled out a lacy handkerchief and handed both to the big hairy thing.

"Is that enough to pay for the flowers and the berries?" asked the old woman.

The big hairy thing examined the apron and the handkerchief. He tied the handkerchief over one floppy ear and hung the apron over the other ear. He shook his head and snorted and laughed and drooled and slobbered and stomped his stinky feet.

Then he stopped and scratched his head. "Uh, what did you ask me?"

"You nasty critter, I think you have berries for brains," fussed the old woman. "I asked if my apron and my handkerchief are enough to pay for the blackberries and flowers! Are they enough?"

"Uh, nope," said the thing. "I think I'll take you home. Maybe we'll eat you for supper, and that will be enough."

The big hairy thing, still wearing the old woman's handkerchief and apron, scooped up the old woman under one fuzzy armpit. Oh, how it smelled! The old woman wiggled and squirmed and pinched that furry arm and pushed herself away from the fuzzy armpit, but she couldn't get free.

The thing stomped farther into the woods, on a path strewn with bones, and into a cave. Farther and farther into the cave he walked. The old woman couldn't see a thing, but she could hear the big hairy thing snorting and sniffling, and she could smell his nasty armpits and stinky feet.

"Oh," said the old woman, "if you were my child, I'd make you take a bath!"

Then the old woman smelled something burning. Soon, the cave seemed to glow. They were moving toward a fire. Here was a kind of cave room, with a fireplace lit, and a dusty, dirty table and chairs all covered with raggedy cloths, and two messy beds. Filthy, bug-chewed rugs covered the cave floor. In the corners of the room were bits of trash and piles of bones. This was the home of the big hairy things!

Standing by the fireplace was Daddy Thing. He was much bigger than his son, and much stinkier. He snorted, *"Snort!"* And he sniffled. And he said, "Fee Fi Fo Fit! What's that hanging under your armpit?"

"Old lady," said his son. He dropped the old woman on the floor and said, "Daddy, let's eat her for supper!"

"You can't have supper in a house as messy as this!" shouted the old woman. She got up, dusted herself off, looked around the room, and saw a broom. She snatched it up and started to sweep all the trash and bones toward the tunnel through which she'd been carried.

"You two take these filthy rugs outside and shake all the bugs and the dust out of them. While you're doing that, I'll sweep the floors."

Big Daddy Thing snorted, *"Snort!* Old woman, I'll eat you right now!"

"No you won't, no you won't!" shouted the old woman. And she batted the bigger hairy thing over his head with the broom, whomp whomp whomp!

"Take these rugs outside and shake them out like I told you, or I'll whack your ears right off your head!"

The big hairy things snatched the filthy rugs from the floor and ran toward the tunnel.

They came back with the rugs well shaken. The old woman had swept the floor and the corners of the cave room. The trash and bones were in an enormous pile on top of one of those raggedy cloths.

"Now, you two take this pile of garbage out and bury it deep enough to keep it from being a problem for anybody," commanded the old woman.

"Uh," said the thing, "Daddy, do we have to do that?"

The old woman walloped his ears with that broom, whomp whomp whomp! The big hairy thing snorted, "Snort!" The handkerchief fell from one of his floppy ears. The apron flew off the other ear and flumped onto the floor.

The big hairy thing and his even bigger daddy wrapped that pile of trash and bones in the raggedy cloth, tied a knot in the cloth so that nothing would fall out of it, and ran for the tunnel again.

It took them a while to dig a deep hole with their crusty claws and bury a cloth filled with so much trash and so many bones. When they returned to the cave room, the old woman had dusted the table and chairs with her own apron. She had set her handkerchief in the middle of the table to make it look pretty.

The old woman had tidied up the whole cave. She'd even made the messy beds.

"There now," the old woman proudly said. "Doesn't this look better?"

"No!" yelled Big Daddy Thing, *"Snort!* This is terrible! What have you *done?"*

"Daddy!" cried the big hairy thing, "Make her go away! Snort. She's ruining our home!

"If we eat her, she might clean up our bellies, too! Snort. Oh, Daddy, make her go away!"

Big Daddy Thing stomped toward the old woman. He growled and snorted and slobbered and drooled. The old woman held up the broom and glared at the thing. Big Daddy Thing stopped and whimpered like a puppy.

"P-p-please, old woman," he begged, "please go away. And take that handkerchief with you. We don't use those things. We just let our noses run, *snort!"*

The old woman smiled. She picked up her handkerchief. She carefully put it into one of the long pockets on her dress. She shook out her apron and dropped it over one arm. She put the broom next to the fireplace. She walked toward the cave tunnel.

But, before she left, the old woman turned to the big hairy things, and she told them, "Now, if you ever see me or anybody else in the woods, you better stay far away. If you don't…

And the old woman reached into another long pocket on her dress and pulled out a comb…

"…If you don't leave people alone…

And she reached into another long pocket and pulled out a bar of soap…

"…If anybody says they have been troubled by you, why, I'll come back here with my soap, and my comb, and I'll scrub you from the tips of your floppy ears all the way down to the bottoms of your stinky feet! Then I'll comb the tangles out of every bit of hair on your entire, hairy bodies!"

"*Aaaaah!*" screamed the hairy things. They hid under the tidy table as the old woman walked away down the tunnel, and onto the path of bones, and into the woods.

The old woman went home. She washed the handkerchief and apron and hung them on the clothesline to dry in the fresh, clean air.

When all that was done, the old woman went searching in the woods for her basket. And when she found it, she refilled it with pretty flowers and blackberries.

And nobody troubled the old woman while she was in the woods. Nobody dared.

NOTES:

I have several "thing in the woods" tales, all rooted in the storytelling of my daddy, Jake Cooper, and my maternal grandfather or "Pop-pops", Byard Wilmer Arkward. He would sometimes begin his versions of folktales with the words "Once upon a time, about time and a half ago".

Yes, I said "Wilmer." I have used his middle name in the story of Li'l Loudmouth. I didn't use it here because Pop-pops never had stinky feet.

This one is an original story, my own variant of something I heard from Daddy or Pop-pops, about time and a half ago, long before I became an old woman.

The Hairy Toe

Retold by Sherry Norfolk

Big Boos

One late fall day, an old woman called Lucinda was digging in the garden. There wasn't much left on the vines or in the ground, but she was hungry and hoping she'd find a carrot or a parsnip that had somehow been left behind. She dug deep, listening to her stomach growl.

Then suddenly, *Chunk!* Her spade had hit something besides dirt! Quickly, Lucinda scraped at the soil, watching as a shape became visible. A potato? That sure would taste good!

She scraped faster, and then, there it was—completely unearthed. It wasn't a potato or a carrot or a parsnip. No—it was a man's great big fat toe, as long as Lucinda's wrinkly hand and twice as dirty. There was a yellowish raggedy toenail on one end, and sprouting all over the front of that toe was a filthy bunch of curly, course brown hair.

"Ugh!" Lucinda dropped the Hairy Toe and backed away from it. Then she turned her back on it, grabbed the spade, and started digging in another spot. But it was getting darker and colder, and she was getting hungrier, and the ground seemed to be empty of anything except that Hairy Toe.

Finally, Lucinda put down her spade and eyed that Hairy Toe again.

Hmmm…it was fat. It was big. It was hairy—yech! But it still had some meat on it. And Lucinda needed some meat!

Lucinda grabbed that Hairy Toe and hurried into the house. While she waited for a pot of water to boil, she shaved the hair off that toe and washed off the mud. Then she plunked the Hairy Toe into the boiling water and added some salt and watched as the Hairy Toe bobbed around the bubbling water.

"Done!" Lucinda proclaimed after a little while. She ladled out her meat and watery broth, added some hot sauce, and gobbled it all down.

"Ahhhhhh," she sighed in contentment. Her stomach felt better than it had in a long, long time. Full and satisfied, Lucinda fell asleep in her rocking chair near the fire.

Thump.

A tiny sound from outside woke her up. She sat up and stretched, listening for the sound to repeat itself.

Thump. Thump. Thump.

It sounded like slow, heavy footsteps…

Thump. Thump. Thump.

And then another sound began, making Lucinda's skin crawl…

"Whoooooo's gooooot my Haaaaaairy Tooooooooe?" a voice wailed through the trees. "Whoooooo's gooooot my Haaaaaairy Tooooooooe?"

Thump. Thump. Thump.

Hairy Toe?

Lucinda dropped to the floor, crawled from window to window, peering out into the darkness. Nothing. Nobody.

"I just had a bad dream—eating a nasty old hairy toe and falling asleep sitting up like that. Just a dream!" Lucinda assured herself. Nonetheless, she made sure that all the windows were shut, and the door was barred.

"Whoooooo's gooooot my Haaaaaairy Tooooooooe?" the voice moaned, sounding closer now.

"Whoooooo's gooooot my Haaaaaairy Tooooooooe?"

Thump. Thump. Thump.

Lucinda looked wildly around her tiny cabin. There was nowhere to hide except a small wardrobe where she kept her meager supply of clothes. Quickly, she threw everything out of it, and climbed inside, holding the door closed as best she could from the inside. She listened…

"Whoooooo's gooooot my Haaaaaairy Tooooooooe?"

That voice was coming from right outside her cabin now…

Thump…creeeeeak…Thump…creeeeak…Thump.

Those heavy footsteps crossed the creaky wooden porch. Lucinda cringed.

Then the voice came again, howling through the door, "WHOOOOOO'S GOOOOOT MY HAAAAAAIRY TOOOOOOOOE?"

BOOM!

The door crashed open, and the footsteps crossed the room.

Thump. Thump. Thump.

Lucinda squinted through a crack in the wardrobe. In the dying fire-light, she could see a monstrous, shadowy, man-shaped figure—and one of its feet was missing its big toe.

Thump.

The monster was right outside her wardrobe now. Lucinda held onto the tiny bolt on the inside of the door as tightly as she could, squinching her eyes shut and cringing…but the door was wrenched out of her grasp… squeeeeeak…

The door slowly opened, and Lucinda stared up at the filthy, hairy, nine-toed thing.

"Whooooooo's gooooot my Haaaaaairy Tooooooooe?"

She watched, wide-eyed, as a long arm slowly reached out towards her…

"I ate your old hairy toe!" she croaked. "You can't get it back, now get out of here!"

The arm stopped…the eyes narrowed…time stood still…

"Got it!"

No one ever saw Lucinda again. Neighbors searched, but the only clue they ever found was a huge footprint out in the abandoned garden. The footprint was missing its big toe.

NOTES:

"The Hairy Toe" is a member of a large family of "Jump Tales" that includes "Tailypo," "The Golden Arm," "The Teeny Tiny Woman," and many more. In his *Treasury of American Folklore* (Crown Publishers, 1944), B.A. Botkin pointed out that these tales "depend almost entirely upon the voice for their effect."

From Mark Twain's "How to Tell a Story,"[5] here's his famous discussion of the correct technique:

> The pause is an exceedingly important feature in any kind of story, and a frequently recurring feature, too. It is a dainty thing, and delicate, and also uncertain and treacherous; for it must be exactly the right length—no more and no less—or it fails of its purpose and makes trouble. If the pause is too short the impressive point is passed, and the audience have had time to divine that a surprise is intended—and then you can't surprise them, of course.
>
> On the platform, I used to tell a negro ghost story that had a pause in front of the snapper on the end, and that pause was the most important thing in the whole story. If I got it the right length precisely, I could spring the finishing ejaculation with effect enough to make some impressionable girl deliver a startled little yelp and jump out of her seat—and that was what I was after. This story was called "The Golden Arm," and was told in this fashion. You can practice with it yourself—and mind you look out for the pause and get it right.

Big Boos love Jump Tales—and it's a mighty satisfying thing for the

---

5 *The Project Gutenberg EBook of How to Tell a Story and Others* by Mark Twain (Samuel Clemens). This eBook is for the use of anyone anywhere at no cost and with almost no restrictions whatsoever. You may copy it, give it away or re-use it under the terms of the Project Gutenberg License included with this eBook or online at www.gutenberg.net

teller to watch them jump three inches off their chairs when that pause is just right!

Capitalize on the strong attraction to Jump Tales to lure kids into the library to find as many variations as possible! Without much encouragement, kids will compare and contrast the stories, evaluating the use of language and how the illustrations add to (or misinterpret) the text. In other words, they will be addressing English Language Arts curriculum standards in a whole and unforced way.

That exploration will naturally lead to more storytelling, which can easily lead to story writing, as kids will want to try their hand at creating their own Jump Stories!

The Gruesome Ghoul

By Sherry Norfolk

"The gruesome ghoul, the grisly ghoul,
without the slightest noise
waits patiently beside the school
to feast on girls and boys."
—Jack Prelutsky, from *Nightmares: Poems to Trouble*
Your Sleep. Greenwillow Books, 1976.

Big Boos

"KEEP OUT," the signs ordered. The signs lined the fence between the school playground and the woods beyond.

"Don't go in the woods," the teachers warned every single time they took their classes out to recess.

"There's an old cemetery in the woods," the kids told each other. "It's haunted—that's why they don't want us to go in there!"

None of the kids really knew what was beyond that fence, but they all had opinions.

"They're *ghouls!*"

"They're monsters!"

"Vampires!" "Witches!"

They laughed at the warnings and made fun of the teachers (behind their backs), but not a single one of those kids ever climbed over the fence to find out what all the fuss was about. Until…

One afternoon during recess, the fourth-grade boys were playing soccer as usual. They didn't have a regular soccer ball, but one of them had brought an old beach ball to school. It was too big and too light and too *cute*—but it was better than nothing.

They filled the beach ball with as much air as it could possibly hold, making it truly bouncy and completely unpredictable. The boys had to learn how hard to kick it (not very) and how high it would fly (really, really) and that it would almost never go in the exact direction they wanted it to go. No matter—the challenge just made the game more interesting.

Naturally, one of the kicks was way too hard and way off-target, and the ball flew over the fence and into the woods. The boys stood and watched it fall out of sight.

"Go get it!" Danny told Mark. "You're the one who kicked it over the fence."

"He can't go get it," Austin said. "He'll get in trouble. We'll all get it trouble!"

"Well, somebody's got to get it," said Seth in exasperation. "That's my big sister's beach ball, and she'll kill me if I don't bring it home."

As they argued, the boys walked over to the fence and peered through the chain links to see if the ball was close enough to pull over with a stick, but it wasn't even visible from where they stood.

"I'm going over," Seth finally declared. "It'll be just inside the woods—I'll be really fast, and the teacher will never even know I was gone."

The boys looked back towards the school—their teacher wasn't looking. They nodded and shrugged, and watched as Seth nimbly climbed up and over the fence, dropping lightly to the ground on the other side.

"Hurry up!" they called, but Seth was already running into the woods.

The ball was nowhere in sight. He began scrabbling through thick bushes and pushing through piles of tangling vines.

"Come on!" his friends urged. Seth was willing, but he couldn't find the ball. How could it have bounced so far? And how could such a big, brightly colored ball be so hard to find?

There! Squinting into the dimness, he finally saw it….lying right between the rotting, decaying feet of a filthy, gruesome ghoul. Seth skidded to a stop, but the ghoul lunged for him, moaning softly, "I'm going to eat your yummy crunchy finnnnnnngerrrrrs…"

Seth tore free, backpedaling and fumbling in his jacket pocket for the peanut butter sandwich he had stored there for snack time. "Here—here! Take this—*eat it!*"

The ghoul grabbed the peanut butter sandwich and shoved it into his gaping mouth. He tried to swallow, but the peanut butter was stuck to the roof of his mouth—and while the ghoul was struggling, Seth kicked the ball away from him and ran for the fence. But the ghoul lunged again, grabbing Seth by the hair and dragging him down to the ground.

"I'm going to eat your gooey, chewy eaaaaaaaaaaarrrrrrs," groaned the ghoul, and he opened his sticky, stinky mouth. Seth reached into his other jacket pocket and pulled out some gummy candy. He shoved it into the ghoul's mouth just in time. The ghoul began to chew…and chew…and while he was trying to unstick the candy from his rotten teeth, Seth jumped up and ran again, scooping up the beach ball on his way to the fence.

The ghoul was right behind him. *Snatch!* "I'm going to squeeeeeeeeeze out your luuuuuuuuungs!" The ghoul wrapped his long, nasty arms around Seth and began to squeeze–"Unh! Uhh! Oof!"

Pop!

The beach ball burst with a sound like a firecracker!

"AAAARRRRRRGGHH! What was *that?*" the ghoul screeched. He dropped Seth and lumbered off into the woods wailing, "Mommmmmmmeeeeeeeeeee!"

Seth didn't waste any time in grabbing the ball and climbing back over the fence. He hit the playground grass just as the bell rang. All of the boys hurried back into the building, pelting Seth with questions.

Seth tried to explain what had happened, but they didn't really believe him. A ghoul? Really? Surrrrrrrre…

Well…maybe…

So every day after that, the boys threw snacks over the fence. And every day, those snacks disappeared without a trace. And the ghoul? Well, that gruesome, grisly ghoul never bothered anyone else again.

NOTES:

Jack Prelutsky's poem about the gruesome, grisly ghoul obviously inspired this story. A portion of the poem is quoted as a prelude to this story. Be sure to read the whole gruesome, grisly poem, found in *Nightmares: Poems to Trouble Your Sleep.* Read it with all the lights on!

The story is based on a very common folktale pattern, easily discerned in stories like *The Gunniwolf* by Wilhelmina Harper (Dutton Juvenile, 2003): an adult warns of danger, the kid ignores the warning, the kid meets up with danger, and the kid gets away safely without resorting to violence. Look at any adventure story, and that basic pattern will be there!

So—make up your own adventure story! Here are the questions to answer:

> ▷ Where will your story take place?
>
> ▷ Who is the kid(s)?
>
> ▷ Who is the adult?
>
> ▷ What danger does the adult warn the kid(s) about?
>
> ▷ What motivates the kid to go into known danger?
>
> ▷ How does the kid get away safely (no violence!)?
>
> ▷ What happens at the end of the story?

You can make the story as scary—or as silly—as you want. It's your story!

CHAPTER 4
SPOOKY SONGS AND SLIMY RHYMES

Bad joke: When does a skeleton laugh? When
somebody tickles her funny bone!

It's a Creepy Night
(Sung to the tune of "Mary Had a Little Lamb")

Adapted by Lyn Ford

Baby Boos and Little Boos

> *Pumpkin faces smiling bright,*
>
> *Smiling bright, smiling bright,*
>
> *Ghosts go flying in moonlight,*
>
> *It's a creepy night!*

> *Trolls and ogres, cats and bats,*
>
> *Cats and bats, cats and bats.*
>
> *Monster masks and funny hats,*
>
> *It's a creepy night!*

NOTES:

Encourage young ones to come up with a two-syllable word that can be exchanged for "creepy" in the last line of each stanza; some possibilities are "spooky", "silly", "crazy", "goofy",…

Enrich the wordplay even further by coming up with other stanzas in which the first three lines follow the presented model: all three lines rhyme; the second line repeats the last words of the first line; the third line is a new statement but still rhymes with the first two lines. Examples:

Mommy's baking pumpkin pie,

Pumpkin pie, pumpkin pie,

Tastes so good it makes me cry,

It's a funny night!

I've got ice cream on my nose,

On my nose, on my nose,

Now it's dripping on my clothes,

It's a messy night!

Did you know that the rhyme, "Mary Had a Little Lamb," an original poem attributed to Sarah Josepha Hale and first published by in 1830, was inspired by something that really happened?

A girl named Mary Sawyer had a pet lamb. At the suggestion of her brother, she brought the lamb to school, causing pandemonium (and probably a lot of squeals and laughter)—ah, what brothers sometimes do to their sisters. John Roulstone, a young man preparing for college by studying with his uncle, the Reverend Lemuel Capen, witnessed the incident, wrote the original three stanza's of the poem, and shared them with Rev. Capen.[6] It is believed that additional lines were composed by Sarah Josepha Hale, but it's possible that Hale wrote the entire poem.[7]

A statue representing Mary's Little Lamb stands in the town center in Sterling, Massachusetts, the place where the lamb incident happened. Mary's school, The Redstone School, which was built in 1798, was eventually purchased by Henry Ford and relocated to the property of Longfellow's Wayside Inn in Sudbury, Massachusetts.

---

6   Roulstone, John; Mary (Sawyer) and her friends (1928). *The Story of Mary's Little Lamb.* Dearborn: Mr. & Mrs. Henry Ford, 8.

7   www.songfacts.com

"Mary Had a Little Lamb" was also the very first recorded verse. It was recorded by Thomas Edison's newly invented phonograph in 1877.[8]

The Wiggle Bug

By Lyn Ford

Baby Boos and Little Boos

The wiggle bug's inside me!

I'm gonna get in trouble.

The wiggle bug won't let me sit still.

It's tickling at my toenails,

It's scratching in my belly.

The wiggle bug is making me ill!

Whenever I get dressed up

Or have to sit politely,

The wiggle bug crawls right into my clothes.

I know I'm gonna wiggle.

I'm probably gonna giggle.

Why, I might even pick my nose!

My grandma's gonna stare.

My Dad is gonna glare.

My Mom is gonna fuss

---

8   Matthew Rubery, ed. (2011). "Introduction." *Audiobooks, Literature, and Sound Studies.* Routledge, 1–21.

And whisper, "Shame, shame, shame."

I'm gonna get in trouble,

And no one will believe me.

That stupid wiggle bug is to blame!

NOTES:

Ask a child to describe a wiggle bug. If the child immediately begins to tell you the creature's characteristics, he or she is probably a linguistic learner. If the child immediately runs for paper and crayons and draws the wiggle bug, he or she is probably a visual learner. If the child immediately begins to show you how the creature moves with gestures and wiggles and squirms and jumps, you've got a "wiggle-bug" or kinesthetic learner standing before you. Well, not *standing*.

If the child tells you, "There is no such thing as a wiggle bug," that child is probably a logical learner, and will question every bit of fantasy you through at him. Lyn seriously doubts that he or she will want to hear about pretend bugs, but stories about the really creepy insects found in your back-yard will fascinate!

And whether the child tells you about the wiggle bug, or illustrates the wiggle bug, or demonstrates the movements of the wiggle bug in its natural habitat, or relates the facts about certain types of insects and their movements, that child is a storyteller. All children are storytellers in their own way.

This poem was created by Lyn years ago, as she thought about her experiences as a mother, a preschool teacher, a classroom tutor, and her own childhood as a wiggly, kinesthetic kid who didn't like to wear dresses and sat still only when reading or drawing or in time out. Any kinesthetic learner can relate to this. Movement is essential as they work and play; it's their way (and Lyn's way) of making sense of the world around them—dance, jump, clap, skip, move, wiggle! This is not acceptable behavior in the classroom, but, oh, how many little children learn in this way!

Lyn feels she may be too old to quickly skip and wildly run they her five-year-old-self did, but, deep in her heart, she is always dancing! And she has no problem dancing like a wiggle bug with large groups of little children, who delight in seeing big people share who they really are.

There are times when we should let our mature, logical mind take a few steps back, put on some music and do a wiggle-bug dance with the little ones!

As an exercise in creativity, cooperatively invent other critters that your children or students might blame for their own youthful missteps. Draw them. Write about them. Laugh at them because they are silly and fictive.

As an exercise in recognizing what's real and what isn't (fiction and nonfiction; "the real story" and a lie), and who is responsible for behavioral outcomes, share the poem, followed by the disclaimer, "This isn't really true. You're smart enough to have figured that out. But isn't it funny that somebody would blame a wiggle bug for their own wiggling?"

The Ghost of John

American (or "traditional English"[9]) folk song, source unknown

Big Boos

Have you seen the ghost of John?

All white bones with the skin all gone.

Oooh, oooh!

Wouldn't it be chilly with no skin on?

Poor old John!

NOTES:

When Lyn was old enough to be a Brownie in the Girl Scouts (oooh, that's so long ago, it's scary!), this was sung as a round. It is as much about sympathy for another's plight, and empathy for another's condition ("wouldn't it be chilly…?") as it is about being haunted by poor John's ghost.

The tune with notations is available (for listening and for purchase) at http://www.musicnotes.com/sheetmusic/mtd.asp?ppn=MN0125371.

---

9   The song is attributed to English folk music at http://www.musicnotes. com/ but I've always been told it was a round as old as the United States, and sometimes sung about the ghost of Tom. The trail of handed-down lore traces the lyrics and tune back to the times of plague in Europe, or to those Europeans who first settled in the Appalachian hills of Kentucky. Somewhere in those tales is the truth of the song.

The Bottom of the Grave
("Sung to the tune of There's a Hole in the Bottom of the Sea")

By Sherry Norfolk

Little Boos and Big Boos

There is slime at the bottom of the grave.

There is slime at the bottom of the grave.

There is slime, there is slime, there is slime at the bottom of the grave.

There's a coffin in the slime at the bottom of the grave.

There's a coffin in the slime at the bottom of the grave.

There's a coffin, there's a coffin, there's a coffin in the slime at the bottom of the grave.

There are bones in the coffin in the slime at the bottom of the grave.

There are bones in the coffin in the slime at the bottom of the grave.

There are bones, there's a bones, there's a bones in the coffin in the slime at the bottom of the grave.

There are flies on the bones in the coffin in the slime at the bottom of the grave

There are flies on the bones in the coffin in the slime at the bottom of

the grave

There are flies, there are flies, there are flies on the bones in the coffin in the slime at the bottom of the grave.

There are maggots with the flies on the bones in the coffin in the slime at the bottom of the grave.

There are maggots with the flies on the bones in the coffin in the slime at the bottom of the grave.

There are maggots, there are maggots, there are maggots with the flies on the bones in the coffin in the slime at the bottom of the grave.

There is slime, there is slime, there is slime at the bottom of the grave.

NOTES

The fun of singing "There's a Hole in the Bottom of the Sea" is trying to remember the sequence, sing the song, and do the actions at the same time. Of course, it gets harder to remember as the song goes along, and everyone ends up flailing around and laughing—including the storyteller!

So…here are the suggested actions (or make up your own) to "The Bottom of the Grave," in the order of the final verse (which, of course, is the hardest!):

- *Maggots*—wiggle pointer fingers like little worms
- *Flies*—with forefingers and thumbs touching, flutter the other three fingers
- *Bones*—arms crossed over chest
- *Coffin*—arms straight out in front

> ▷ *Slime*—wipe hands together

> ▷ *Bottom of the grave*—point down, down, down.

Practice first—it's a challenge!

Antigonish (I met a man who wasn't there)

By Hughes Mearns

Big Boos

> *Yesterday, upon the stair,*
>
> *I met a man who wasn't there*
>
> *He wasn't there again today*
>
> *I wish, I wish he'd go away...*
>
>
> *When I came home last night at three*
>
> *The man was waiting there for me*
>
> *But when I looked around the hall*
>
> *I couldn't see him there at all!*
>
> *Go away, go away, don't you come back any more!*
>
> *Go away, go away, and please don't slam the door...(slam!)*
>
>
> *Last night I saw upon the stair*
>
> *A little man who wasn't there*
>
> *He wasn't there again today*

Oh, how I wish he'd go away...

NOTES:

Although many people think that this poem has only one stanza and no title, or that the author is the prolific "Anonymous," the author is actually William Hughes Mearns (1875–1965), who was better known as Hughes Mearns.

The poem "Antigonish," inspired by reports from Antigonish, Nova Scotia, of a male ghost roaming up and down the stairs of a haunted house, was written in 1899 for an English class. It was introduced to Lyn by her father's recitation of the first lines whenever she was discovered hiding on the stairs and watching something she wasn't supposed to view on television (usually something scary, or a late-night film noir). Her mom would fall asleep on the sofa, and Dad would come home from work and find Lyn trying to quickly tiptoe back up the stairs. Rather than awaken Mom, Dad would recite, in soft and deep, slow syllables, the verse that would haunt Lyn's attempts to sleep more than the guilt of disobeying her mother: "Yesterday, upon the stair…."

Yeah, Lyn says her dad was weird. Loving, but weird.

Hughes Mearns was a Harvard graduate, an educator, and poet. His ideas about encouraging the natural creativity of young children were considered interesting in his day, when they were ahead of his time. He listened, really attentively listened to little ones.

And he wrote poems like "Antigonish."

Weird. Brilliant, but weird.

Create a parody of any stanza with your kids. Examples from Lyn:

As I was sitting in my chair

I saw my cat in underwear

I don't know how he got that way

I just wish that she'd go away

Or

When I came home from school at three,

My baby brother spit on me.

But when I yelled so Mom would know,

He disappeared! Where did he go?

This is a poem that can bring up conversations about what really scares us, both as children (Big Boo-aged readers, please) and adults. It can open a door to sharing empathetic conversation, creating a bond that will be cherished and remembered. Lyn remembers the poem with fondness, but she remembers the moments of hearing her father's deep voice share it with love and an affectionate sense of connection to him.

Information about Mearns was gleaned from the website https://en.wikipedia.org/wiki/William_Hughes_Mearns and Mearns' book, *Creative Power: The Education of Youth in the Creative Arts Paperback,* second edition, February 1958, from Dover Publications.

Stirring Her Brew

By Sherry Norfolk

Baby Boos

There once was a witch

Who had to make a brew.

The trouble was,

She didn't know what to do!

She built a big fire

And put a cauldron on top

She filled it up with water,

Then she came to a stop.

"What goes into

my bubbling brew?

Help me, please!

I don't know what to do!"

[Let children tell you what to put in, such as spider legs, bat wings, etc. As each suggestion is made, pretend to throw it in a pot.]

She put it all in

And she got her big spoon

She began to stir,

She began to croon:

Stirring and stirring and stirring her brew

Wooooo! Woooooo!

Stirring and stirring and stirring her brew

Woooo! Wooooo!

Stirring and stirring and stirring her brew

Woooo! Wooooo!

Tip-toe, tip-toe, tip-toe

BOO!

NOTES

Long ago in Sarasota, Florida, Sherry was a preschool teacher. Halloween was their favorite time of year, and this was their favorite song/chant (it can be either or both). She and her students always gathered in a circle, pretending that a huge cauldron stood before each of us, and that we each had great big spoons to stir our nasty concoction.

No matter how many times they did it—and they did it many times—the kids never tired of coming up with new ideas for ingredients—frog eyes, lizard lips, cockroach legs. Then they would begin the chant…howling to the right and howling to the left: Wooooooo, Wooooo!

Verrrrrry quietly Sherry and her Little Boos would tip-toe towards the middle: tip-toe, tip-toe, tip-toe…

Then spin around and shout, "BOO!"

Since those long ago days in Sarasota, Sherry has used this chant every Halloween, gathering new groups of Baby Boos around her and stirring up brew. It takes some practice and some coaching. The kids are usually very excited the first time, but, of course, they don't know what's going on. They'll mimic the adult's actions, and be very surprised on the Boo! Then Sherry whispers conspiratorially, "Let's practice—we can scare your mom (or teacher)!"

Sherry points out that participants stir three times, and tip-toe three times. They practice the verses, with Sherry holding up her fingers to help them count the repetitions. They go faster and faster on the "Stirring and stirring…" part, but quieter and quieter on the tip-toeing part, then jump and spin to shout BOO!

After a few practices, they can make the teachers or parents JUMP!

Queen Nefertiti

Anonymous

Big Boos

Spin a coin, spin a coin,

All fall down;

Queen Nefertiti

Stalks through the town.

Over the pavements

Her feet go clack,

Her legs are as tall

As a chimney stack.

Her fingers flicker

Like snakes in the air,

The walls split open

At her green-eyed stare;

Her voice is thin

As the ghosts of bees;

She will crumble your bones,

She will make your blood freeze.

Spin a coin, spin a coin,
All fall down;
Queen Nefertiti
Stalks through the town.

NOTES:

When sharing this rhyme, Lyn suggests creating a little English Language Arts lesson as well as a lot of physical activity: Copy and print out this verse. Read it together in a choral presentation, so that the sounds of the words and the flow of the actions are clear. Assist participants in looking up or figuring out any words they don't know or understand. Then tell your young participants to underline all the action verbs. Discuss and model movements that add meaning to these verbs. Then encourage participants to create their own movements to display the actions, and reread or recite this creepy verse using the newly adopted movements.

There's also an Ancient History lesson in researching Queen Nefertiti, an Egyptian Queen and wife of the pharaoh, Akhenaten.

This poem can be found on page 203 of Jack Prelutsky's and Arnold Lobel's *The Random House Book of Poetry for Children*. This collection, first published by Random House in 1983, is still an amazing source of poetry for the child's heart in each of us.

The Worms

Big Boos

Did you ever think, as a Hearse goes by,

That you might be the next to die?

They'll dress you up in a long white gown

And bury your body beneath the ground.

And the worms crawl in

The worms crawl out

The worms crawl everywhere

Round about

Then each one takes

A bite or two

Of something or other

That used to be you.

And the worms crawl in

The worms crawl out

The worms crawl everywhere

Round about

And your eyes fall out

And your teeth decay

And that is the end of a perfect...

Day

NOTES:

This is a PC version of a much longer, much more gruesome traditional song. Sherry used to sing it with the group of kids who gathered after school every day at the North Dade Regional Library in Miami, Florida. They shivered and shuddered and giggled and gagged and begged to do it again!

If You Ever See a Monster

(Sung to the tune, "Did You Ever See a Lassie")

Author Unknown

Baby Boos and Little Boos

If you ever see a monster,

A monster, a monster,

If you ever see a monster,

Well, here's what you do!

Make this face......

And that face.....

And this face.....

And that face.....

If you ever see a monster...

Be sure to shout...BOOOOO!!!!

NOTES:

Obviously, this is one of those preschool songs that gets passed around and passed around until nobody remembers where it was first heard. Lyn heard it at an early childhood education conference back in the 1980s. That's all she remembers, but she has been singing the song with Little Boos ever since. The best part is making the faces!

The Twelve Nights of Trick or Treat

(Sung to the tune of "The Twelve Days of Christmas")

Adapted by Lyn Ford

Little Boos and Big Boos

> *On the first night of Trick or Treat*
>
> *Somebody gave to me*
>
> *A bat flapping 'round a dead tree—Yuck!*

> *On the second night of Trick or Treat*
>
> *Somebody gave to me*
>
> *Two crazy crows*
>
> *And a bat flapping 'round a dead tree—Yuck!*

> *On the third night of Trick or Treat*
>
> *Somebody gave to me*
>
> *Three freaky frogs*
>
> *Two crazy crows*
>
> *And a bat flapping 'round a dead tree—Yuck!*

> *On the fourth night of Trick or Treat*
>
> *Somebody gave to me*

Four stinky toes

Three freaky frogs

Two crazy crows

And a bat flapping 'round a dead tree—Yuck!

On the fifth night of Trick or Treat

Somebody gave to me

Five screaming ghosts! AAAAAH!

Four stinky toes

Three freaky frogs

Two crazy crows

And a bat flapping 'round a dead tree—Yuck!

On the sixth night of Trick or Treat

Somebody gave to me

Six greasy goblins

Five screaming ghosts! AAAAAH!

Four stinky toes

Three freaky frogs

Two crazy crows

And a bat flapping 'round a dead tree—Yuck!

On the seventh night of Trick or Treat

Somebody gave to me

Seven rotten apples

Six greasy goblins

Five screaming ghosts! AAAAAH!

Four stinky toes

Three freaky frogs

Two crazy crows

And a bat flapping 'round a dead tree—Yuck!

On the eighth night of Trick or Treat

Somebody gave to me

Eight Jack-o'-lanterns

Seven rotten apples

Six greasy goblins

Five screaming ghosts! AAAAAH!

Four stinky toes

Three freaky frogs

Two crazy crows

And a bat flapping 'round a dead tree—Yuck!

On the ninth night of Trick or Treat

Somebody gave to me

Nine slobbery ogres

Eight Jack-o'-lanterns

Seven rotten apples

Six greasy goblins

Five screaming ghosts! AAAAAH!

Four stinky toes

Three freaky frogs

Two crazy crows

And a bat flapping 'round a dead tree—Yuck!

On the tenth night of Trick or Treat

Somebody gave to me

Ten monsters moaning

Nine slobbery ogres

Eight Jack-o'-lanterns

Seven rotten apples

Six greasy goblins

Five screaming ghosts! AAAAAH!

Four stinky toes

Three freaky frogs

Two crazy crows

And a bat flapping 'round a dead tree—Yuck!

On the eleventh night of Trick or Treat

Somebody gave to me

Eleven zombies groaning

Ten monsters moaning

Nine slobbery ogres

Eight Jack-o'-lanterns

Seven rotten apples

Six greasy goblins

Five screaming ghosts! AAAAAH!

Four stinky toes

Three freaky frogs

Two crazy crows

And a bat flapping 'round a dead tree—Yuck!

On the twelfth night of Trick or Treat

Somebody gave to me

Twelve creaky doors

Eleven zombies groaning

Ten monsters moaning

Nine slobbery ogres

Eight Jack-o'-lanterns

Seven rotten apples

Six greasy goblins

Five screaming ghosts! AAAAAH!

Four stinky toes

Three freaky frogs

Two crazy crows

And a bat flapping 'round a dead tree—YUCK!

NOTES:

This is obviously a takeoff on "The Twelve Days of Christmas", a cumulative English carol that was first published as a rhyme in the 1780's

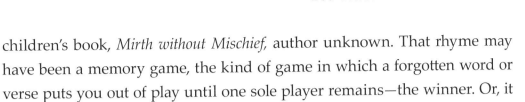

children's book, *Mirth without Mischief,* author unknown. That rhyme may have been a memory game, the kind of game in which a forgotten word or verse puts you out of play until one sole player remains—the winner. Or, it may have been a "forfeit game," in which the player who makes a mistake or forgets the line must give up something like a cookie or perform a favor— such as a kiss.

The song has become an ongoing exercise in mathematical appraisal. Since 1984, the cumulative costs of the gifts mentioned in each verse have been used as an economic indicator. If each verse's items are counted, a total of 364 gifts are delivered by the twelfth day of Christmas. In December of 2011, the total cost of repeated gift sets was listed as $101,119.84. Now, there's an opportunity for a math lesson!

To view the article and "Christmas Price Index" chart, go to "The 12 Days Of Christmas—A Lesson In How A Complex Appraisal Can Go Astray" at http://www.fulcrum.com/12Days_Christmas.htm

A WORD TO THE WISE

For those little ones who shouldn't have heard a certain story, or seen a certain movie, or heard the evening news, or whose vivid and creative imaginations have made bedtime a scary moment, there are some concrete possibilities to make that moment a little easier to face. Keep in mind, their fear is real, and it's not helpful to deny it. Also, it's dishonest to tell a child there are no monsters, then come into the room and shoo something out of the closet or from under the bed. Instead, try a few fun exercises, like:

- The spin-around: Turn clockwise three times and say, "Turn around, turn around, ghosties and creepies. Go away, go away, I'm getting sleepy.

- Monster Sprays and Monster Swatters: An empty spray bottle filled with colored water, a fly swatter in a bright color, can be means of self-defense and independence! Create a special kit for your little one, and tell them that monsters hate the spray, and go away. But if they don't go away fast enough, the Monster Swatter will chase them away. Please note: I didn't say *hit* the monster. As a former preschool teacher, that's one word I try not to use, ever.

- Miz Kathryn's way: Beloved storyteller Kathryn Tucker Windham was famous for telling ghost stories. Her "Jeffrey" was and is a favorite ghostly character among storytellers who knew and loved Miz Kathryn. But she didn't want her listeners to lose any sleep over her tales, so she always gave this bit of advice: If you don't want to be bothered by ghosts, simply place your shoes side by side, pointing in opposite directions, beside your bed. The ghosts will be confused about whether you're coming or going, and they'll go haunt someone else.[10]

10   *Alabama Ghosts and Jeffrey,* by Kathryn Tucker Windham. Strode Publishers, 1969.

RESOURCE LIST

The following books contain stories that are often told or read to young listeners—but whether or not they are "age-appropriate" for your listeners is a very subjective decision, and one that only you can make!

Boos for Baby Boos

Bright, Robert. *Georgie.* NY: Scholastic, 1990.

Brown, Ruth. *A Dark, Dark Tale.* NY: Dial, 1981.

Carter, David A. *In a Dark, Dark Wood: An Old Tale with a New Twist.* NY: Little Simon, 2002.

Emberley, Ed. *Go Away, Big Green Monster!* NY: Little, Brown and Co., 1992.

Galdone, Paul. *The Teeny-Tiny Woman.* NY: Clarion, 1984.

Hicks, Barbara Jean. *Monsters Don't Eat Broccoli.* NY: Dragonfly Books re-issue, 2014; originally Alfred A. Knopf, 2009.

Howe, James. *There's a Monster Under My Bed.* NY: Atheneum, 1986.

Mayer, Mercer. *There's a Nightmare in My Closet.* NY: Dial Books for Young Readers, 1968.

Mayer, Mercer. *There's Something in My Attic*. NY: Dial Books for Young Readers, 1988.

Sendak, Maurice. *Where the Wild Things Are*. NY: Harper & Row, 1963.

Williams, Linda. *The Old Lady Who Was Not Afraid of Anything*. NY: Crowell, 1986.

Boos for Little Boos

Cole, Joanna. *Bony Legs*. NY: Scholastic, 1983.

Galdone, Joanna. *The Tailypo: a Ghost Story*. NY: Houghton Mifflin, 1977.

Mayer, Mercer. *Liza Lou and the Yeller Belly Swamp Monster.* NY: Four Winds Press, 1976.

Mitter, Matt. *I'm Going to Eat You!* White Plains, NY: Reader's Digest POP edition, 2006.

O'Malley, Kevin. *Velcome*. London, UK: Walkers Children's Books, 1999.

Rockwell, Anne. *The Bump in the Night*. NY: Scholastic Paperbooks, 1980.

San Souci, Robert D. *The Boy and the Ghost.* NY: Simon and Schuster, 1989.

San Souci, Robert D. *The Hobyahs*. NY: Delacorte Press, 1994.

Wahl, Jan and Wil Clay. *Little Eight John*. NY: Lodestar, 1992.

"Wait Till Martin Comes" in Goode, Diane. *The Diane Good Book of American Folk Tales & Songs*. NY: E.P. Dutton, 1989.

Sierra, Judy. *The House that Drac Built*. San Diego: Harcourt Brace, 1995.

Wood, Audrey. *Heckedy Peg*. San Diego: Harcourt Brace Jovanovich, 1987.

Boos for Big Boos

Bang, Molly Garrett. *Wiley and the Hairy Man: Adapted from an American Folktale*. NY: Macmillan, 1976.

DeFelice, Cynthia C. *The Dancing Skeleton*. NY: Macmillan Publishing, 1989.

Haskins, James. *The Headless Haunt and Other African-American Ghost Stories*. New York, NY: HarperCollins Children's Books, 1994.

San Souci, Robert D. *Even More Short and Shivery: Thirty Spine-tingling Tales*. NY: Delacorte, 1997.

San Souci, Robert D. *More Short and Shivery: Thirty Terrifying Tales*. NY: Delacorte, 1994.

San Souci, Robert D. *Short and Shivery: Thirty Chilling Tales*. Garden City, NY: Doubleday, 1987.

Schwartz, Alvin. *Ghosts! Ghostly Tales from Folklore*. NY: HarperCollins, 1991.

Schwartz, Alvin. *In a Dark, Dark Room and Other Scary Stories*. NY: Harper & Row, 1984.

Schwartz, Alvin. *More Scary Stories to Tell in the Dark*. NY: Lippincott, 1984.

Schwartz, Alvin. *Scary Stories 3*.   NY: HarperCollins, 1991.

Schwartz, Alvin. *Scary Stories to Tell in the Dark*. NY: Lippincott, 1981.

Van Allsburg, Chris. *The Widow's Broom*. Boston, MA: Houghton Mifflin, 1992.

Additional Boo Resources for Boo Tickle Tellers

Beaulieu, Trace. *Silly Rhymes for Belligerent Children*. Marine St. Croix, MN: Amorphous Productions, 2010.

Bowers, Sharon. *Ghoulish Goodies: Creature Feature Cupcakes, Monster Eyeballs, Bat Wings, Funny Bones, Witches' Knuckles, and Much More! A Frightful Cookbook*. North Adams, MA: Storey Publishing, LLC, original edition, 2009.

Brown, Marc. *Scared Silly! A Book for the Brave: Poems, riddles, jokes, stories, and more*. Boston, MA: Little, Brown and Company, 1994.

Dahl, Roald. *Roald Dahl's Book of Ghost Stories*. NY: Farrar, Straus, Giroux, 1983.

Forgey, William. *Campfire Stories…Things That Go Bump in the Night*. Merrillville, IN: ICS Books, 1985.

Goode, Diane. *Diane Goode's Book of Scary Stories & Songs*. NY: Dutton Children's Books, 1994.

Hamilton, Martha and Mitch Weiss. *Scared Witless: Thirteen Eerie Tales to Tell*. Little Rock, AR: August House, 2006

Jones, Jennifer (ed.). *The Ghost & I: Scary Stories for Participatory Telling*. Cambridge, MA: Yellow Moon Press, 1992.

MacDonald, Margaret Read and Roxane Murphy. *When the Lights Go Out: Twenty Scary Tales to Tell*. Bronx, NY: H.W. Wilson, 1988.

Olliver, Jane. *Kingfisher Treasury of Stories #02: The Kingfisher Treasury of Spooky Stories*. Boston, MA: Kingfisher, a Houghton Mifflin Co. imprint, 2003.

Reiner, Carl. *Tell Me a Scary Story…But Not Too Scary!* Boston, MA: Little, Brown Books for Young Readers, 2007.

Reiner, Carl. *Tell Me Another Scary Story…But Not Too Scary!* Beverly Hills, CA: Phoenix Books, 2009.

Young, Richard and Judy Dockery. *Favorite Scary Stories of American Children*. Little Rock, AR: August House, 1990, 1999.

Questions & Answers With Authors
Lyn Ford and Sherry Norfolk

1. Why would you write a book of creepy stories for little kids?

Sherry: Little kids *love* to be just a little bit scared—especially when they are surrounded by friends and teachers and all the lights are on! In a safe environment, children are able to master fears and difficult experiences by reinventing them in a playful way. Scary stories have the potential to support children's development by allowing them to vicariously meet and overcome danger while remaining firmly and completely safe.

Lyn: "Creepy" can simply mean "weird." It doesn't have to refer to anything disturbing or horrible. Children like weird stuff (if you've ever watched some of their cartoon favorites, you already know that), especially when it can be appreciated and shared with humor by the big people they trust. In the October, 2001 issue of *Child* magazine, reporter Patti Jones said, "…scary tales serve an important purpose, say psychologists and children's literature specialists…[providing] great entertainment [and helping] kids through key developmental stages…fairy tales actually help kids face the fears they already have—and vanquish them."

2. What were your criteria for including a story or verse?

Lyn: I've been working with children since I was a thirteen-year-old Sunday-School teacher. That was 1966, the same year that *It's the Great Pumpkin, Charlie Brown,* based on the Charles Schulz' comic strip, Peanuts, was televised for the first time (in my birth month, October!). It was beautifully sweet and silly, safe and family-oriented, mildly spooky and somewhat creepy, and a cross-generational event that parents and children could enjoy together and talk about after the program ended. That became the criteria for stories written or selected for this book.

Sherry: Forty years of working with children as a teacher, librarian, storyteller and teaching artist, plus a lot of reading of educational psychology and child development research, informed the process of story selection. After all, as a performing artist, I have to make those decisions on a daily basis by answering some of these questions:

- ▹ What is age-appropriate for this audience?
- ▹ What will delight them?
- ▹ What will captivate them?
- ▹ What will make them shiver?
- ▹ What will make them laugh?
- ▹ Is the vocabulary suitable?
- ▹ Are the images accessible?
- ▹ Are there multiple opportunities for participation?
- ▹ In other words: WILL IT WORK?

3. For whom is this book written?

Sherry: *Boo-Tickle Tales* are not-so-scary stories just right to be told or read to young listeners, Pre-K through fourth grade. Our book is written for the kids—and for the storytellers, parents, grandparents, teachers and caregivers who will share the stories with them.

Lyn: The book is deliberately structured so that parents and mentors can select options *for* their young listeners (aged 3 or 4) and *with* their young readers (aged 4 or 5 through 9), and share *together*. We've also included resource information and tips for the tellers, whether they're family members presenting in the comfort of their homes, or media specialists and other storytellers presenting from the stage.

4.   **What educational value is there in such stories?**

Lyn: Educational standards in English Language Arts and other areas of study require the mastery of skills in critical thinking, speaking and listening, pre-reading, reading, and writing. Reading and telling folk-tale and fairytale types of stories, as well as narrative adventures developed in original stories, creatively model and approach these skills. Rhymes and songs and repetition in actions offer higher level language skills in formats that act as tools and frameworks for remembering and recreating ideas. It's all brain-building fun!

Sherry: *Boo-Tickle Tales* are carefully crafted to meet the emergent literacy needs of young listeners. The tales for the youngest are full of repetition, which is helpful for comprehension, vocabulary acquisition, predicting, and sequencing. They have been written or adapted to offer a wide variety of interactive options, making them accessible for all learners. They're *fun*—researchers have found that children need to hear 1,000 stories before they can learn to read (Mem Fox, *Reading Magic* [Harcourt, 2001]). *Boo-Tickle Tales* motivate kids to listen to stories and to learn to read! The stories for older children provide many opportunities to develop skills such as visualizing, problem-solving, predicting and inferring, and vocabulary-building—all essential to comprehension.

5.   What experience do you both have with sharing such stories?

Sherry: I began telling boo-tickle tales to three-, four- and five-year-olds when I was a preschool teacher in the mid-70s (Halloween was the kids' favorite time of year!). I continued to tell them, expanding my repertoire to include age-appropriate material for school-age children, middle school, high school and adult audiences, as a children's librarian, and then Children's Outreach Coordinator for the Miami-Dade Public Library. As a full-time storyteller for the last 20 years, I have told boo-tickle tales to thousands of children in preschools, elementary schools, botanical gardens, museums, and festivals nationally and internationally.

Lyn: Sherry and I were both preschool teachers, and the month of October was all about getting ready for Halloween. I've been telling age-appropriate stories for that season (although requests now often come for "harvest-time" programs, the stories are still spooky!) since 1972, and as a professional storyteller since 1993, with an ever-increasing repertoire that now includes something for all ages and listening skill levels. But I started early, around the age of ten, telling stories to my siblings and cousins, and they still remember.

6.   Tell us a bit about responses you've received to sharing such tales. What was the feedback from children, parents, or mentors?

Lyn: My favorite response was a proposal of marriage from a five-year-old boy who wanted me to come to his house and tell more "spookies." I thanked him for liking the stories, and told him I was already married, so I couldn't marry him, which elicited a shrug and "Okay." As he ran to the library books, his mother walked up to me and said, "I wish I could take you home with us. This was so much fun, and I want to hear more stories!" Other favorite responses are gained by listening to program participants repeating phrases and rhymes from the stories, or talking about the stories as they leave the venue.

Sherry: Invariably, the response from parents and mentors is, "That

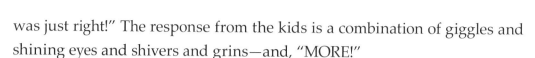

was just right!" The response from the kids is a combination of giggles and shining eyes and shivers and grins—and, "MORE!"

7. How did you respond to such stories when you were a child?

Sherry: Cuddled with my brother on my grandfather's knee, it was delightful to allow myself to visualize not-so-scary situations and be absolutely certain that they would either be safely resolved—or my grandfather would keep US safe! As we got older, we entered the "That couldn't really happen!" stage—constantly testing our emerging understanding of the world against the fantasy worlds in the stories. And then—completely confident that we knew fact from fiction (but preferring the make-believe world over the mundane one)—we sought out and read those stories for ourselves.

Lyn: I loved spooky stories!!! Dad told them with his naturally deep voice, and I could see everything he said—every character, every setting, every scene. I would listen intently, and safely wander on a journey into the unknown and back to the security of home, knowingly guided by my father, my favorite storyteller. I asked for the same stories again and again, which is probably why I still remember some of them.

8. What's with the bad jokes???

Sherry: Most of our "bad jokes" are puns—a type of wordplay that requires children to think about words from different points of view, to dig beneath the surface a bit to find the hidden meaning. Aside from the vocabulary-and comprehension-building value of this, they are just plain fun!

Lyn: I collected these jokes and others—puns, knock-knock jokes, and goofy questions with nonsensical responses—every time I told spooky stories at the Columbus (Ohio) Zoo or our local libraries. I wrote them down because they were so "bad" that they were funny, but I never told them; I'm a good storyteller, but a very poor jokester.

9.   Why did you feel the need for this book in spite of the many that are already on the market?

Lyn: After a program of Boo-ticklers (a name I coined for the gentler tales I'd tell in the little kids' part of the "Grave Tales" library program in Dublin, Ohio), a father asked me if I had written down any of my silly but slightly spooky stories. He and his teenaged son had come for the program for older participants, but they'd arrived early enough to listen for something he might safely tell to his younger children when they asked for "scary" stories. This dad said, "Your stories are just enough, *just enough*. If you write that book, I'll buy it!" We wrote that book.

Sherry: While there are many collections of scary stories for 4th graders and up, there are far fewer for our target audience (ages 3-9)—and most of those were not written by storytellers! As storytellers, we are able to craft tales that "fit in the mouth"; that is, we crafted tales that read aloud smoothly and naturally, and are brought to life through the spoken word.

10.   What's your next writing project?

Lyn: I'm at the outlining stage of a collection of folktales and other stories to nurture empathy and socio-emotional development. That manuscript doesn't even have a title yet. Then I'd like to put together a few more stories and a bit of folklore from my Affrilachian family. Seems like I've become the story-heritage keeper, and I've got a lot of research to do.

Sherry: Two projects are in the beginning stages right now: a book on community programming and community-building through youth storytelling in libraries, after-school groups, etc., and a book on the uses of storytelling in the Special Needs Classroom.

If you have enjoyed the telling—and
discussion of—not-so-scary stories for children,
please take some time to visit:
http://www.storytellerlynford.com
http://www.sherrynorfolk.com
http://www.parkhurstbrothers.com
http://www.storynet.org